JEAN-PIERRE,

UNLOCK YOUR POTENTIAL!

10 Golden Keys to Success

YOU ARE CALLED FOR GREATNESS!

SOAR HIGH!

LOVE,

Francois

DR FRANCOIS ENGELBRECHT

With Dr Elmari Marais

What others are saying about FRANCOIS ENGELBRECHT

If you are tired of earning your average income, having average joy in life and accepting average performance, it is time to meet Dr. Francois Engelbrecht. His warm personality, motivational enthusiasm and passion for life, inspires all to greater heights.

- Dr Christa van den Berg
Moderator and International Counsellor (South Africa)

If you are looking for a true spiritual father, sharp teacher of the Word of God and excellent business coach,you should meet Francois who is living it, both in church and in the business world.

- Professor Paul Kilundu
Entrepreneur and Academic (Democratic Republic of the Congo)

Dr. Francois Engelbrecht is a respected, reputable and professional coach for people across the world. He is filled with revelatory wisdom from God that he applies in everyone's unique circumstances. He has the gift of providing clear direction in your personal and business life. While he focuses on your unique gifting, he helps you to become accountable for your own success. His passion is to see people free from the bondages of the past so that they can fulfil their goal in life. If you have the chance to work with him, do not think twice!

- Hanli Marais

Entrepreneur, Life Coach, Business Coach and Business Owner (South Africa)

The passion Francois has for assisting people to reach their full potential, is amazing. He will provide you with a strategy to find the gold in you and to lead you to higher heights. I would not be where I am today, had it not been for Francois Engelbrecht.

- Meshack Aswani
Leader and Entrepreneur (Kenya)

Francois lives to unlock the potential in others to reach their dreams. He wants to see people become successful in all areas of their lives. As a colleague and friend, I highly recommend Francois as coach for your personal life and as an entrepreneur to attain wealth.

- Mark Loretz
Entrepreneur, Life Coach, Business Coach (South Africa)

My connection with Francois was supernaturally planned. I was at a point in my life where I had a big decision to make. With his guidance, I started my own business and through him, I have reached so many of my goals. My understanding of market place ministry has totally changed. If you want to take your business to the next level, or if you want to overcome some obstacles, Francois Engelbrecht can help you.

- Jonathan Peters
Entrepreneur and Business Owner (Nigeria and South Africa)

Dr. Francois is one of the humblest people I know. For more than a decade, he has fulfilled the role of father, mentor and friend. He had a deep impact on my life. I can truthfully say that I am where I am in my life as result of his influence and passion to empower people. I have seen how he has influenced leaders worldwide, so that they too can realize their dreams.

- Ivan van Niekerk
Leader (South Africa)

I have known Francois for the past 18 years. When you meet him, he leaves a lasting impression. He really cares about you and always brings direction to your life in a caring manner. He speaks the truth in love and you feel at ease in his presence. He awakens the God given dreams inside you and helps you believe that you can realize them. If you want a life changing experience, I strongly encourage you to connect with Francois for a coaching session.

- Cilliers Coetzee
Entrepreneur and Business Owner (South Africa)

“What others are saying about ELMARI MARAIS”

I am privileged to know Dr. Elmari Marais as a colleague and long-time friend. She is a people's person filled with passion for those in need. She is an intelligent, highly qualified and outstanding business woman. Elmari is a talented and a sought-after musician and she has an exceptional gift for writing. She is an anointed speaker and teacher who captivates audiences and shifts paradigms. With her sharp humour and wide general knowledge, she brings flavour to any group. I am privileged to know Elmari and I'm indebted to her for the hours of translating.

- Dr. Francois Engelbrecht
Business Coach, Entrepreneur and Academic.

By reason of my walk with Dr Elmari Marais throughout the past four years, I can strongly recommend her for her outstanding character. I have known Elmari to be firmly grounded. Integrity and faithfulness mark her traits. She is a compassionate songwriter and musician who truly captivates an audience. As an author of books and poems, she made her mark and touched many hearts. She carries a strong anointing to inspire audiences through public speaking. She is definitely a respected person who is called to pass on the baton to generations!

- Johanna Carstens
Leader and Business Woman.

Dr. Elmari is a multi-gifted woman of God: a business woman, anointed poet, writer and passionate speaker. Her love for God and His people are evident to many in the Body of Christ. I not only recommend her books, I recommend the author too.

- Meshack Aswani
Leader and Entrepreneur (Kenya)

A woman gifted with many talents, she has an extraordinary gift in her writing style. She speaks through her poetry about God's glory, holiness, intimacy and His Love for His children. She is a balanced and sensitive matured woman of God.

- Dr. Zoë Grobler
Leader and Prophet

Dedicated to my seven grandchildren

Migael, Jean, Franco, Anke, Estie, Kaylah and Kiara.

May you soar high on the winds of success

and experience complete fulfillment.

Published by Power Books, Cape Town, South Africa.
Design & Print: Maverick Media SA
+27 21 30 3460 | info@maverickmedia.co.za

UNLOCK
YOUR POTENTIAL
10 Golden Keys to Success

FOREWORD

On many occasions I have been confronted with these questions: "Why are you so busy with so many things at the same time? Why do you do these things?"

My answer is simple.

Life is exciting when you have discovered who you are and what you live for! It is one big adventure to be involved in so many things! The ultimate highlight is to see how a person's potential is unlocked, their happiness increased and their lives fulfilled.

On the other hand, it is one of the saddest experiences to travel through Africa and to see how poverty swallows up our continent, while Africa is one of the resource richest continents in the world! There are so many opportunities around us to help build financial success, if we just know where to look and what to do.

What if someone could pick up this book and, while paging through it, have one sentence jump out at him or her? What if that sentence had such an impact that the person cannot help but be drawn to read the whole story? And what if he or she discovers ten keys to success that help them get on their feet and discover the riches within to help build financial prosperity?

As people apply the principles in the book, their lives slowly but surely start changing course, like a big ship on the ocean. Changes in marriage; no more strife about money; work environment changes; changes in their finances. After a few years the extra money from other streams of income flows into their bank accounts. A decade later, and they are financially free to live life and do what they have always dreamt of.

But what if the reader decides to sow this book into the life of someone else who is struggling to keep afloat. He or she may decide to journey with this person and help him or her to build his/her future. Help them see the silver lining and pursue their dreams with hope.

This is why this book is in your hands. My desire is that it will inspire you to experience and pursue true success, abundance and significance, and then share it with others.

Enjoy!

Dr. Francois Engelbrecht

INTRODUCTION

The three shots ring out in quick succession. They fly passed the tin shack where Shafik's eyelids blast open, smashing his dream and pulling him from his deep sleep. He is paralysed with fear. His heart beating in his throat, his body frozen in time, waiting to hear if the shots were aimed at him or someone else. But it suddenly goes very quiet and the tension in his muscles slowly lessens.

These rude awakenings are nothing new in the township where Shafik lives. Gangsters marking territory, removing those who do not dance to their tunes. You can count yourself lucky if a stray bullet does not pierce you, you are not caught in the crossfire and you make it to the next morning.

Shafik glances at his watch. Its 04:40 and he knows he will not be able to go back to sleep. Maybe a hot cup of coffee will help to restart his day.

Shafik was born in a poverty-stricken suburb on the Cape Flats. His mom was an eighteen-year-old girl from a rich suburb. When she fell pregnant with Shafik, her family sent her packing, renouncing her. His father was a young man who came from India to try and build a new future for himself. The most these two young lovers could do for themselves, was to build a makeshift one-roomed shack on "the Flats" and furnish it with second hand pieces: a bed, a table and a chair.

Remember the stray bullets? His father was not so lucky. He was killed in the crossfire between two rival gangs when Shafik was only five years old. Difficult times were to follow. His mother had to stretch her meager salary to provide for Shafik and his younger sister.

And under these conditions, the young Shafik spent his formative years. Poverty was everywhere. Small children played outside while their parents tried to earn some money to buy the basic necessities. Young adults, who had left school before finishing their schooling, but had no opportunity to study, could be found just hanging around, selling drugs and getting swallowed up by gangs.

With the steaming cup of coffee in his hand, Shafik for a moment, puts away the thoughts of his father's untimely death. He has to get ready for his first day as a waiter at a popular local restaurant. The steakhouse is located in a rich neighbourhood against the backdrop of Table Mountain in Cape Town. Now it was time to put into practice what he had learnt during his training. He knew he was ready, but the butterflies in his stomach still made him feel jumpy.

With his neat apron and his name glistening on his chest, he steps up to meet his first customer. The man, in his late forties, exudes confidence. He surely is a businessman. With a wide smile, Shafik leads the man to a table, and offers him something to drink. The man must be a regular as he does not hesitate to order, without glancing at the menu. While he eats and reads the newspaper, Shafik stands at a distance, watching him. He notes that the man has his vehicle keys, mobile phone and tablet neatly stacked on the table at his right-hand side. Shafik is somehow in awe of what he sees, yet he cannot pinpoint exactly what it is that is holding his attention.

Once the man was done , Shafik greets him, breathing a sigh of relief that all went well. Little was he to know that this man would come to play a pivotal role in his life.

Three months later, Shafik's client walks in and their interaction more or less follows the same pattern as the previous one. With one exception. While cleaning the table after the man had left, Shafik finds ten R100 notes under the serviette. His insides turn cold and he feels a slight sweat on his brow. A R1000! His mind starts racing. Just think what he could do with so much money! And surely no one will notice if he quickly slips it into his pocket! He finds himself looking around to see if anyone else has spotted his find.

With a sigh, he stops his own thoughts and pulls himself together. A thief? That is not who he is. He walks over to the manager to report what he has found. Luckily, they have the man's number and promptly inform him of the misplaced notes. When the man collects the money the next day, he slips his business card into Shafik's hand with a message.

I will mentor you to be successful: for free.
Contact me if you are interested.
John Wiseman.

Shafik stares at the card, his heart beating wildly. He cannot believe it! Is this the chance he has been hoping for?

The day drags on as Shafik longs to get home so that he can call Mr Wiseman. Some of the other waiters have told him that Mr Wiseman is a professor of neurology and that he is a billionaire with shares in many businesses. But to Shafik, he just looks like an ordinary man; like any other businessman in Cape Town.

That night, with trembling fingers, Shafik punches in John Wiseman's number on his mobile phone. It just rings. Shafik leaves a nervous message, not having much hope that the man will phone back. An hour later, John phones back and makes their first appointment.

Mr Wiseman's office is on the eigth floor and overlooks the Atlantic Ocean. Shafik sinks into the comfortable leather chair as they sit across from each other. He clutches the hot, freshly made coffee in his hands.

John senses Shafik's nervousness and tries to keep the conversation light and exploratory. He tells Shafik a bit about his background.

Shafik certainly can identify with the struggles of poverty. John's father worked for the railroad company and he grew up in a small village alongside the railway tracks. After finishing school, he had to find work. There was no money for further studies. He started as a clerk in the bank and saved enough money to start his first year medicine at university. He excelled at his studies and was awarded scholarships from his second year onwards. He specialised in neurology and was appointed as lecturer soon after he finished his community service.

While working and studying, he also started his first small business: buying and selling good quality second hand clothes on Saturdays at a flea market near the beach. And so, he started gaining financial experience in the bank, business experience with his micro enterprise and learned about the brain during his years at university. Today, he is a successful professor in neurology as well as a successful businessman with various businesses.

John Wiseman knew what it was to be given a chance. His thankfulness led him to want to share his success and he therefore decided to choose a willing student with whom to share the principles he had learnt.

Shafik was one of those "finds" that he wanted to see succeed.

Too quickly, the visit reaches its end and they decide to meet each other for an hour every third week for a mentoring and coaching session. John has already indicated that he wants to teach Shafik about ten important keys that will help him to unlock his potential. After revealing each key, Shafik would have to do some homework before their next meeting and the first few minutes of the following session will then be spent on feedback on the assignment. Doing things increases the speed of change and John is set on helping Shafik change his future until success becomes a normal part of his life.

I. THE PINK BRAIN

It is a beautiful spring day in the Cape. From where he is sitting, Shafik can see the variations of blue of the ocean with a few freight carrying ships making their way to the harbour.

John is wearing a light blue shirt and neat pants. As he leans back in the leather chair, he looks intently at Shafik. "What is your biggest dream in life? What do you want to achieve, Shafik and where do you see yourself in ten years time?"

Shafik has dreamt about it so much that he does not even hesitate to answer.

"I want a good job, a beautiful home and my own vehicle, Sir. A man must be able to provide well for his wife and children."

"That is a very good answer, Shafik. But let's start off on the right foot. We are going to spend at least the next three years working together. I would like you to call me 'John'. Otherwise, we may struggle to become friends!"

"That will be difficult for me, Sir...eh, John. I was not raised to address people older than me by their first names. But I will try!"

John's smile plays around the corners of his mouth. How he understands where this kid comes from.

"Now that we've got that out of the way, let me tell you about this." And with that, John opens his hand to reveal a spongy pink plastic brain. He places it on the coffee table and a moment's silence rests between them. Shafik stares at the brain, seeing the deep folds all over it, the two halves clearly on either side of what looks like the Rift Valley.

John breaks the silence, and startles Shafik as he points to the brain and says, "The power of thoughts. The brain is mightier than the combined power of a host of computers. This is the place where our thoughts are birthed. From our thoughts, our words flow which translate into actions. The brain almost works like the fuel tank of a vehicle. Your vehicle will either sputter uphill or fly up depending on what fuel you have put inside that fuel tank. Did you know, that each morning you wake up, this machine has generated new brain cells?

Shafik softly replies, "No Mister John" already forgetting to call John by his first name. "I just heard that you lose brain cells as you grow older."

John chuckles. "That's true, Shafik, but the good news is that we do have those fresh, new ones every morning and we can choose what we do with them. Are we going to fill our brains with positive thoughts, filled with hope for a great future, or are we going to poison them with negative thoughts and words? When you have that positive outlook, it helps this computer on your shoulders to do all things necessary to obtain what you dreamt of: the job, the house, the vehicle."

Shafik's eyes are fixed on the plastic brain which has since moved from the coffee table back into John's hands. Something deep inside Shafik is stirring. An excitement he has not felt since...well, since forever. His brain can help him achieve what he has been dreaming of? He has not even shared all of his deepest desires with the Professor. Like owning his own business, or travelling the globe, or helping children raised in poverty to truly live!

John's soft voice pulls him back to the conversation.

"It's a bit like riding a bicycle. Do you remember your first time, Shafik?"

Shafik laughs and nods his head in confirmation. He remembers very well how much skin he lost as the bike slid from underneath him. But he did manage to learn how to ride, albeit with bleeding knees!

"The first few times you had to concentrate real hard to peddle and balance all at the same time. After a few tries, your brain started learning how things worked and you could start cycling without even thinking about the basics. In just the same way, your brain learns new thought patterns with repetition. And this is how we change the course of our future."

"So, what you are saying is that my dream about my future does not just have to stay a dream? But how will I be able to change from where I am at and where I've come from, to that place I have dreamt about? Surely it is not just going to help thinking positively? What must I do to taste success?"

"I am glad you asked, Shafik," John picks up the brain from the table and rolls it around in his hands.

"That is exactly why we need to walk this road together for the next three years. Nothing worthwhile, happens overnight. It is going to call for dedication and hard work; two golden rules that not everyone understands or has the guts for. But I can promise you this: as we work through the ten keys of success, and train ourselves, we will grow and will achieve our dreams."

Shafik lets his gaze rest in John's eyes. He knows they have reached a pivotal point. A point where he will have to decide whether he is going to trust the process, and John.

"Will you teach me?" Shafik's voice has an urgency in it and it surprises him. "I want to know how my brain works; how it can help me achieve what I am dreaming about!"

"Young man, of course! Your breakthrough starts today! Your enthusiasm is contagious! There are those who say that it takes 21 days to change a negative from your past into a positive. So, let's start with you going home and writing down your dreams. If you have pictures, paste them next to your dream. Then, for the next 21 days, every morning and evening, speak out loud positive thoughts about these dreams. Believe that you will achieve each one and watch what happens in future! Do you know, that studies have shown that when you speak things out loud, it will come to pass three times quicker than when you only think it? Wonderful, isn't it!"

Shafik's head feels as if it wants to explode with excitement. Finally, he has something to do!

"Bring your dream book along next time we meet. And, then, after that meeting, you can start professing the dreams. I first want to show you something interesting."

"No problem, Mister John!"

"And just one more thing, Shafik: things change in life when you change."

"What is that supposed to mean, Mister John?"

"The more you work to better yourself, the easier success follows. It is important to read the right books, to attend conferences, to study those that have reached great heights. Start applying what you have learnt so that it becomes second nature to you. Work harder on yourself than you are working at your job."

"Books? What books should I read? What conferences? Whom should I study? Though I have already started studying you..." Shafik shyly adds.

"Try Caroline Leaf's book, 'Switch on Your Brain'." John reaches over to his book shelf, takes out the book and hands it over to Shafik. "You can have my extra copy until you can buy your own."

With determination, Shafik says, "I'll start right away. I want to understand this machine on my shoulders."

John bursts into hearty laughter.

"I like you and your determination. The most successful people on earth have never stopped learning. A formal qualification might get you a job and provide an income, but that which you learn along the way, brings wealth. That is what I mean when I want you to start reading and researching successful people."

"May I ask you a personal question, Mister John?"

John nods in anticipation.

"How many books do you read in a year?"

"I aim to read at least one book a week, but with my full program, I am lucky if I manage two a month. I do, however, like to keep abreast with my subject field of neurology. But I also try reading about business, adventure and whatever interesting subject I can find. When I have not read in a while, something inside me starts yearning for it. That is why I keep my electronic library close at hand, for those moments I can just manage to read a few sentences."

Shafik seems spooked. The most he has read was maybe three or four books a year. This will be a tough task.

"Shafik, you can start off slowly by trying to read a book a month. You will notice how you start growing in the year ahead."

Shafik feels better. One book a month feels more within his reach.

"Can you believe it, Shafik? Our hour is up. Here is a gold chain. I trust you will carry it with you because next time I will give you a key to put on the chain. And remember to bring along your dream book and come and tell me what you have learnt from that book on the brain that I'm lending you." John says as he gets up from the easy chair.

Shafik is beaming.

"I will see you soon, Mister John. Thank you for your time, the gift and the book! I cannot wait to start reading it."

With a handshake, the odd couple greet each other. Shafik is trembling with excitement and he wants to burst into song, but is mindful of his presence in a fancy office environment. In the elevator, he carefully takes the gold chain out of his pocket and hangs it around his neck.

2. DYNAMITE WORDS

Just after 14:00 Shafik arrives on campus to meet Professor Wiseman at his office. Most of the morning classes have been finalised and it's no wonder Shafik sees students relaxing on the green grass or sitting chatting under the trees on park benches. Shafik arrived early to give himself enough time to find the Professor's office.

The door stands ajar and while his hand curls around the door knob, he hears John's friendly greeting.

"Welcome on campus! Excellent students like yourself always leave this place with more knowledge than they arrived with."

Shafik smiles as he shakes John's hand. He gazes around the office. Two of the walls are covered with shelves containing rows and rows of books. The other wall has a massive screen where digital information can be displayed. On his desk, Shafik notices family photos and two scale models of the brain.

John offers him an ice-cold juice and as they each grab a seat, he slowly pushes his dream book across the table towards John. John looks like a cat who has just received a bowl of full cream milk. The brain book follows suit.

"That was a great read, Mister John! I could not put it down. I just had to go and buy my own copy. There are so many new things I learned that I wish to apply to my own life!"

John, with a broad smile on his face, pushes a small box across the table in Shafik's direction. Shafik cannot contain his curiosity, and as he opens it, he sees a gold key partly hidden in the black velvet. It has the word **"THOUGHTS"** engraved on it. In a flash, he remembers their discussion on how thoughts play such a vital role in success. He carefully takes out the key and threads it onto the gold chain.

"So, what stood out for you in the brain book?" John asks with interest.

"I guess the brain's ability to change. I think it was called 'neuro plasticity'? I could not believe what an impact negative, toxic thoughts could have on our health and life! But I was thankful to read that positive thoughts can help you grow your brain. I don't think I will ever be able to, well, think like I used to!"

John sees how Shafik's excitement is just bubbling over. This teaching certainly had a big impact on this young man.

"Shafik, how about we take what you've learned a step further?"

Shafik nods and his smile gives John all the consent he needs.

"Let's look at what 'dynamite words' can do."
John closes the curtains, and turns off the office lights. With a remote, he points to the screen and it flashes on. It suddenly it feels as though Shafik is in his own private cinema.

A busy street appears with people scurrying across it, each heading in his own direction - fast. The camera picks up a blind man sitting on the pavement. In front of him, there is a tin in which people can donate money. In his hands, he holds a sign that reads: 'I am blind. Please help!' The people, who look like ants running to and fro, pay little attention to the man. It is almost as though he is invisible to them.

Shafik starts feeling edgy. Why doesn't anyone help the man? Then, a lady stops. She pulls out a thick black pen, takes the sign, writes on it, and leaves. Suddenly, people start reacting. Some even stop to speak to the man before they drop coins in the tin. As the camera zooms in, Shafik can see how the words were changed: 'It's a beautiful day...but I cannot see it'.

Shafik is still pondering the power of the previous sketch, when another one appears on screen. It shows a Japanese doctor, Dr. Masaru Emoto, a scientific researcher, busy cooking rice. He places the cooked rice in three separate jars and seals them. He then proceeds, for the next 30 days, to say out loud to the first jar, 'Thank you!', to the second, 'You idiot!' and to ignore the third jar. After 30 days, the rice in the 'Thank you!' jar was still pearly white. The 'You idiot!' jar's rice had, however, turned dark and mouldy and the rice in the 'ignored jar' started to rot! The test proves that words have dynamic power when they are released into the atmosphere.

The creak of John's chair as he gets up to open the curtains brings Shafik back to the room.

"Never in the history of mankind have so many words been used as is the case in this day and age. Just think of the impact of social media and the internet, the increase in technology and the super technology in your mobile phone. With positive words, good news can be distributed, excellent information can be shared and a lot of money can be made. But with negative words, people's lives can be destroyed. And the saddest part is: once you have spoken that negative word, you may be able to apologise, but you cannot take it back. It is like a fluffy pillow with duck feathers that you shake out in the wind. Even if you try, you will not get those feathers back into the pillow."

Shafik's head has dropped.

He softly starts recalling his life.

"Where I stay, I see this play out the whole time. Small children's lives are destroyed by a drunk mother yelling and screaming at them for no reason and fathers that tell them they are 'no good'. These same children and others end up in gangs to try and fit in, to protect themselves. There are women walking around in misery, black and blue because they serve as a punching bag for their husbands. I wish they could have seen what you have showed me today..."

"But you are here today, Shafik. You can start making the difference. It is so simple: just start writing down short affirmations of what you want to see and be and speak it out aloud: daily. It has a positive impact on your brain as it helps to change brain patterns. It is almost as if you give your brain a fitness workout. 'Feel-good' hormones are released, and the brain starts forming new neuron groups with positive thoughts. In the brain, it looks like little trees forming new branches. When we do this regularly, the positive patterns start to overtake those negative patterns that you have been nurturing for years, without realising it. Can you see how the art of using words wisely and correctly is so important for our lives?"

"That's is exactly what I read in the book. Our brains physically change, and we are healthier when we start thinking and speaking positively. But how does a 'positive affirmation' work, Mister John?"

John smiles as he points the remote to the screen again. On the screen the following words appear:

In one year's time I am starting my own business and one day I will have many successful businesses.

"This is an example of a positive affirmation, Shafik. It is a short, positive thought I have written down and which I say out loud often. It affirms my dreams and ambitions and helps me to believe that what I am uttering, is possible. When you write it down and start speaking it, it puts your brain in motion to plan how you are going to reach your dreams."

"Do you still have such affirmations that you wrote down and are speaking, or did you just do it while you were on your way to achieving your dreams, Mister John?"

"Throughout my life, I have written down these affirmations. And I still do it to this day. When I have reached a goal, I can remove that affirmation from my list, with much gratitude! But, you know, Shafik, life is so full of adventure that there are always new dreams that I can write down and speak out loud. Sometimes, those affirmations come true in the same year I first wrote them down. This is such a powerful tool!"

In the dimmed office, the two men sit in comfortable silence.

"Are there more tips you can give me about these affirmations, Mister John?"

"Many years ago, I discovered a book that has so much power locked up inside of it, that I use it every day of my life. In actual fact, my life changed irrevocably the day I met the Author. In one place in the Book, He promises that He will fulfil every promise in the Book. And now I use quotes from this Book with my affirmations and it gives my words power!"

John can sense Shafik's interest rising. Almost as if there is an electrical current hanging in the air, just waiting to earth somewhere.

"Mister John? What book and author are you referring to?"

"The Bible, Shafik. I only discovered the power of the words in the Bible the day I personally met God. Remember the affirmation I showed you on the screen a while ago? With the Bible, that affirmation changes slightly to include a promise from the Bible:

In one year's time I am starting my own business and one day I will have many successful businesses. Because with God, all things are possible!

Shafik shifts uncomfortably in his seat and it's almost as though he doesn't know where to look. "Maybe we can talk a bit about your God later..."

John senses his discomfort and changes the subject.

"It is important that we truly believe what we have written down, Shafik. It also will not help if we speak the affirmation, but later on speak negatively about our dream. All my words must speak life into and over what I believe. Do you think you can try this?"

In his heart, Shafik knows that if he does not try this, his life is likely to remain as it is: stuck in a township in a zinc hut, working crazy hours as a waiter, depending on tips for his livelihood. For this reason Shafik utters a 'Yes!'.

"That is great, Shafik. You can take your dreams and use them as a basis to start writing affirmations. Paste it to a wall you walk by so that you can speak them out loud every morning and evening until it is a reality. Got it?"

"Yes, Mister John! That seems simple enough. I don't have anything to lose. When is our next meeting?"

"Let's do something different next time. I will meet you at the entrance to the Cape of Good Hope Castle, then we can go for coffee inside a part of history."

As Shafik walks to the taxi rank under the leafy green tree lane on campus, he is deep in thought. The things he heard today have given him much to chew over. He stops at a fountain and for a brief moment sits down. There are so many questions spinning in his head, but then there are other things Mister John mentioned that are just as logical. And the fact that Mister John is so successful, means that he must be doing something right! Maybe he should give that Book a chance as well...even if it was prohibited in his religion.

3. OLD CASTLES

Shafik spots John waiting for him with two tickets in hand to enter the Cape of Good Hope Castle in Cape Town. They are both glad to see each other and the conversation starts immediately when they are within earshot of each other. Shafik is in awe of the castle's thick and high walls built by slaves so long ago. It must have been almost impossible to penetrate these walls in the days when the castle was a fort for the Dutch East India Company in the 17th century.

"And, how did you get on with writing those affirmations, Shafik?"

"Very well in fact, Mister John! I slipped up only two mornings when I was running late for work, but otherwise, I have been affirming my dreams every morning and evening as you suggested. I...I also had a long, hard think about that Book you mentioned. I want to try it, Mister John. But I need your help getting the right passages to fit with my affirmations."

"Any time, son! May I see what you have written?"

Shafik gives John a piece of paper with his affirmations neatly typed out. Shafik has also searched and pasted appropriate pictures alongside each affirmation.

"Well done! I am truly impressed, Shafik. This is so neat and very well written! Where shall I write down the verses for you?"

"Thank you, Mister John. I have left spaces under each affirmation, so you are welcome to fill it in. I have everything on my computer, so I will just add what you write down."

John starts writing and soon Shafik's affirmations take on a more detailed form:

- *Within six months I will have a new job with a better salary and in three years' time I will have my own business. Because my God shall supply in all my needs according to His riches and glory in Christ Jesus (Philippians 4:19).*
- *Within one year I will have my own apartment and within five years I will own my own house because all things are possible for him that believes (Mark 9:23).*
- *Within nine months I will own my first vehicle. Ask, and it will be given to you (Matthew 7:7).*

"How does that sound to you, Shafik?"

"That sounds right, Mister John! Maybe one day I will be the one to add the Bible verses," Shafik says, eyes twinkling.

John manages to hide the slight moistness in his eyes as he shifts another small box across the table towards his friend. It contains another key, this time engraved with '**WORDS**'.

John may have tried to hide his tears, but Shafik is less successful. As he holds the key in his hand, he feels the tears starting to well up in his eyes and he struggles to swallow his emotions. John is starting to feel like that father he has been longing for; someone that genuinely cares and encourages. He just feels so at home with John that he actually does not even care if John sees his tears.

After what seems like a lifetime of quality silence between them, it is John who breaks the silence.

"How much money did you have growing up?"

Shafik's stares at the movement of the spoon as he slowly stirs the sugar in his second cup of coffee. It's when he looks up into John's eyes, that John sees a bit of what this young man went through.

"It was tough, Mister John. There were days when we did not even have anything to eat. I had to go to bed hungry. There was just no hope for any future. And the fact that everyone around us went through the same thing, did not help. I just thought that that was how life should be. Even today, I am one of the few ones who actually has a job and who brings enough home so that our family can eat."

With empathy, John listens. And still his emotions want to bubble over.

"That is unimaginable, Shafik. Do you think it is possible that you will become a rich man one day?"

His head hanging, Shafik speaks without looking up. "That's what I want to believe so that I can help others, but right now, I am not sure. If I look at my background, I really don't know if I will be able to do it."

John reaches across the table, placing his hand softly on Shafik's arm. This is the first time he has felt compelled to touch Shafik, except when they have shaken hands.

"Listen to me: that is exactly why we have met and why I suggested that we meet at the castle."

"What do you mean, Mister John?"

"Look around you, Shafik. In the time that the castle was built, do you think the enemy could attack it easily from outside?"

Shafik takes a look around and again sees the high and thick walls. He sees the places where the guards would have stood with their weapons to defend the castle from the wall should the enemy try and enter. And then he sees the place where the canons were mounted to stop any advancing enemy from a distance.

"Well, it doesn't look like it would have been easy to enter. This place looks strong and a handful of soldiers would have been able to defend it from high up on the battlements."

"You're spot on, Shafik. This fort was a powerful one in the early years of the Cape of Good Hope. How you think about your poverty background can be just as strong in your mind, as this castle was in reality."

The deepening frown on Shafik's forehead shows John he may have to do some more explaining.

"Shafik, let's start again with the brain."

John extracts a small blue plastic brain from his pocket and places it between them.

"The brain works with association. If it has thought about something once, it is logical to think about it the same way the next time that situation arises. It is almost as if that first thought creates a footpath. If you have a herd of cattle and you place them in a new camp, they will hang around for a while. But when they become thirsty, they will sniff the air for water and the leader will start moving towards that water source. And the rest follow. After a few weeks, the pathways are clear and when it's drinking time, they will use that same footpath over and over again."

"Our brains work in a similar fashion. What you have thought and learnt from a young age, determines how you see life. And if you have grown up thinking there is a lack of money, that message will be stuck in your subconscious to this day. Can you see how this can become like a strong fortress or castle constructed in your thought life? And it is not so easy to enter into that castle and break it down."

"But how do I break them down, Mister John? It seems I have a few fortresses in my mind."

"Shafik, of course there is a way. We can take that fortress and later on, completely demolish it. But it does take hard work and strategy. Just like the enemy who wanted to attack and take over this castle needed to strategise and fight hard."

"I get it, but I need your help!"

"Remember what you read about those neuron groups that look like little trees that form in your brain? You and I need to start planting new trees, ones that believe that there is hope and a great future for you. And we have to focus not to feed or water those castles or trees from your background so that they can die off."

With a chuckle, Shafik says, "So, it sounds that we are about to start a nursery in my brain! Where do we start, Mister John?"

"Maybe we should start with believing. Wealth is centred on a certain way of thinking about finances. Just like poverty is a certain way of thinking about finances. Poverty is always scared that there will not be enough at the end of the month. It will stand with bowed head and open hands to beg for more from other people, because you are not convinced that you can provide for yourself. Poverty does not easily give to others because it is scared that there will not be enough left. Even rich people, can have a poverty mindset if they want to hoard money and can never get enough. But that discussion on wealth and riches we will tackle some other time. For now, we need to start believing and speaking positively about your financial future."

"Now that you have learnt about the castles in your mind, is there possibly another affirmation that you would like to write down, Shafik?"

"Yes, if you would help me with a verse out of your Book? Because you said that the verses always come true?"

John smiles, "Of course. It is the Author of the Book who makes the verse come true and I will certainly help you. What is your affirmation?"

"I believe that I will be a successful businessman and that I will become very rich one day."

"Wonderful!" John answers. "Maybe you can insert: Because God gives me the strength to obtain riches. That comes from Deuteronomy 8:18".

"Is that really written in your Book? Does your God really want us to be rich?" Shafik asks in awe.

"Yes, Shafik. God is a father and wants to give His children only the best. He cares for His children."

While Shafik adds the affirmation and scripture to his list, he is deep in thought about what he has just heard about God. A God who is a father? That wants only the best for them? Never in his life has a heard about such a God.

As he finishes up, John asks, "Shafik, may I ask you a personal question?"

Shafik nods.

"Do you have any debt? Do you owe anyone money?"

Shyly, Shafik nods. "I had to buy new clothes to wear to work and I needed taxi money. So, I borrowed R3000 from my friend. And I have to make sure there is food at home. The money that comes in, flows out so quickly. I can see my friend is anxious about his money and I will have to repay him soon. Luckily, I am doing well at work, so my plan is to start next week paying him a small amount each week."

"And what are your thoughts about debt, Shafik? If you need something again, and you do not have the cash, will you contact your friend now that you know, with your job, you are able to repay him?"

The silence is heavy between them.

"I really don't know, Mister John. If someone wants to lend me money so that I can get ahead in life, I might just do it again."

John reaches into his bag and pulls out a pair of handcuffs. He places it next to the blue brain. Shafik's has seen how the police slap similar cuffs on law-breakers before driving them off in the police van.

"Shafik, debt is made by lending money from a friend or a bank. This type of debt usually goes along with the payment of interest on the money you borrowed. That is why debt is like handcuffs that ties your hands behind your back. There are certain types of debt most people do enter into early in life, like when you buy a house or a vehicle. But, debt is always dangerous. Think of it as a loaded pistol. It has the potential to hurt you and others. Therefore, it is best to turn your back on the temptation to buy things when you do not have the money for it. Rather start exercising patience and wait a bit longer until you have saved enough. It is also the cheaper way of buying!"

"You're right, Mister John. I feel terrible having had to ask my friend for money. It almost feels as though it has harmed our relationship. What do you suggest? What is the quickest way for me to get out of debt?"

John looks intently at Shafik before answering.

"There are a few things to remember, Shafik. Firstly, acknowledge that you have debt and that it has to be paid back as soon as possible. Then, you need to be responsible to someone, so I would suggest a life coach who can help you set up an action plan to get debt free. Draw up a budget so that you know exactly what you need to spend money on. 'Debt payment' should be part of your expenses until it has been paid off. Try to set aside 20% of your monthly income to target that debt. And, as we have been learning, you need to speak life over your finances, everyday!"

"Wow, Mister John, that is a mouthful. I may need to ask you again to list those steps for me. Would you be willing to be my coach? Or does your schedule not allow it?"

John packs the handcuffs and blue brain in his bag.

"Shafik, I will coach you free of charge and we can work it into our sessions when we see each other. Will you start a basic budget and bring it along next time we meet? If you get stuck, you will find some workable examples on the internet. I also want you to bring a suggestion of how you will get out of your debt and stay out of debt."

"Got it! I will bring it along next time, thanks!" Shafik eagerly replies.

"O, by the way, Shafik," John adds while they are getting up to part ways. "I have spoken to three of my business friends. The one is in the banking industry, the other in mass maize trade and the other in the import and export of fruit. All three indicated that they are prepared to look at your CV. Their offices are all here in town. If you're interested, get your CV ready. You are welcome to send me your first draft before you send it off to my friends."

John digs into his shirt pocket and hands over a folded piece of paper with the contact details of the owners. Shafik seems frozen in time. John chuckles and refolds the contact list, takes Shafik's right hand and folds his fingers around the paper.

"I don't know what to say, Mister John. I have been looking for a new job opportunity where I can grow. Maybe this is it?"

And then John does something Shafik will never forget. Instead of the usual outstretched right hand to greet, John pulls him in a tight embrace, like a father would embrace a son. As John releases his grip, he looks Shafik in the eye and says, "I know you will make a huge success of your life!"

Shafik looks down at his shoes. The emotions inside all bottleneck in his throat and his vision starts to blur as tears start spilling over. Long after John has left, Shafik still stands at the coffee table. He wonders whether this is really happening to him or whether he is back in his shack, dreaming.

4. A LIFE OF ABUNDANCE

Shafik cannot get home quickly enough. He feels so motivated to upgrade his CV. At 01:30 the next morning he feels confident enough to send his CV to John to check. He falls into bed filled with a feeling of accomplishment. His body wanted some sleep, but his mind kept churning on the events and words spoken at the castle.

Just before work, Shafik takes a peak at his emails. Low and behold, John has already answered his email with suggestions to improve the layout and contents. Quickly, Shafik completes the amendments and sends the finished product off to the three business owners.

To his surprise the feedback from the business owners was quick. All three wanted to see him! The interview at the bank was a bit intimidating and he was interviewed by three people. They asked him questions about his job history and his current job as a waiter at the restaurant. They also tried to gauge his level of financial awareness and why he would want to pursue a career in banking. . Though he tried to answer as best he could, he could not help but feel a bit disappointed and unsure as to whether that could be classified as a 'good interview'.

Two days later, he had another interview with the maize retail manager. Shafik walked into that interview knowing that he had very little background of the industry. Somehow, however, he felt more at home in this environment than with the previous interview and he was less nervous. Maybe that was because he had learnt from the previous one.

That evening, while Shafik is cooking supper, his phone rings. It's John, phoning to hear how the interviews went. Shafik shares his experiences thus far and John advises him to read up on imports and exports before he walks into his final interview. A few days later, Shafik receives a short, but professional email from the bank, thanking him for his application, but that there are currently no vacancies. They will, however, hold onto his CV should future vacancies become available. Shafik slowly closes his laptop screen. There is a nauseating feeling in the pit of his stomach. He has been rejected. But, the feeling does not last too long. He knows he did his best in that interview and he will continue doing his best. His interview tomorrow will be successful!

The day of the third and final interview has arrived. Shafik is nervous as he walks into the offices of Delicious Fruit, the import and export company. Waiting in the foyer Shafik sees an office door swing open and a man with a broad smile walks towards him with an outstretched hand.

"You must be Shafik. It is good to meet you! Welcome to Delicious Fruits! I am Danny, the Managing Director."

Shafik falls over his words to get the necessary pleasantries out of the way. Once seated in Danny's office, the interview starts, but it goes much further than the standard questions Shafik has had to answer in his previous two interviews. Danny is very interested in his long-term plans and dreams. When Danny asks Shafik about his lively interest in imports and exports, Shafik feels as though his words have become a waterfall. His passion just tumbles over his lips as he recalls what he has read about the industry and what he thinks it means for the South African economy.

As they walk out, Danny extends his hand to Shafik and says, "So, when can you start?"

The colour drains from Shafik's cheeks. He was not expecting that!

"Well, I could probably start next week, but that might not be fair to my current employer. May I have an extension to work

out my last month as waiter before I start here?"
Danny is even more impressed.

"Of course, Shafik! It is always good not to burn bridges. One never knows when or if your path will cross with your current employer in future. Congratulations on your new job! Please ensure that you see our human resources manager, Mrs Jansen, before you leave today. She will finalise your starting date and contract, and the rest!"

Shafik is overwhelmed.

"Thank you, Sir. I really appreciate this opportunity. I will not disappoint you!"

"Shafik, from what I have seen and heard, I know you will try your best. I believe that we will work well together."

Mrs Jansen is in her mid-forties, extremely neat and very professional. She explains to Shafik in detail the company procedures and what would be expected of him. Once they have decided on a date to start Shafik leaves with a handful of notes. Outside, he cannot help but skip the last three steps, pumping his fist and yelling, "Yes, yes, yes!" as he flies through the air.

He grabs his mobile phone and calls his mentor, Mister John, to share the brilliant news and to make a date for their next meeting.

It is late Friday afternoon when Shafik meets John at the clock tower in the Cape Town harbour. Both are dressed in casual clothes as John suggested and Shafik has his rucksack with overnight necessities. He has no idea what John is up to.

John is also carrying a small rucksack and they start walking towards the harbour. John waves to someone on a luxury yacht and the person steers the vessel to berth alongside them. He throws out a big rope that John deftly wraps around a cement pillar on the pier. Next, a walkway is swung from the yacht and John motions to Shafik to step onto the yacht.

Shafik shuffles across. It is his first time on a yacht. The yacht leaves the harbour, and the adrenaline starts pumping as the first waves hit. They stand at the prow of the yacht and he can feel the sea spray on his face as he clutches the steel railing. The wind ruffles their hair and as he whips his head around to try and get it out his eyes, he notices a school of dolphins next to the yacht. He excitedly pulls John's arm and points at the beautiful creatures accompanying them. Now and then, a dolphin jumps out of the water and re-enters like an Olympic diver.

Soon, the Mother City has been left far behind and the captain lets down the anchor in the deep ocean. The crew bring out deck chairs, fruit juice and snacks while the sun is slowly being swallowed up by the ocean.

Shafik cannot get enough of this beauty and already has taken a boat load of photos with his mobile phone. But he knows that those photos will never bring to life what he is experiencing right now.

"Congratulations with your appointment, Shafik. I am very proud of you!" John cannot keep the excitement and pride out of his voice.

"How did it go with your attempt to set up a budget? And did you bring it along?"

"Thanks, Mister John! Yes, I brought it. It's in my rucksack. If you'll excuse me just a moment." Shafik disappears below deck to the sleeping quarters. Soon, he is back with his neatly set out budget and some notes.

"I first started with what my finances look like at this moment and included my debt. Next to it, I drew up another budget based on my new job and salary. That certainly looks better, doesn't it, Mister John?" Shafik asks proudly.

"It was a bit more difficult to get out of my debt than I thought. But you will see that I really took away all the niceties to ensure that I can spend 20% of my income on my debt. There will be enough left to help my mother. With this new job, I can be financially free sooner. What do you think, Mister John?"

"You did a great job, Shafik. This way, and if you stick to this budget, you will settle your debt very soon!"

With that, John removes a little box from his hooded jacket. Again, it contains a golden key, this time inscribed with **"CASTLES"**. Shafik eagerly takes the key and places it alongside the other two on his chain.

"Do you have any idea why I brought you out here on the ocean to overnight, Shafik?"

"Not the foggiest idea. I was hoping you would tell me," Shafik says with a broad smile.

"Look around you, Shafik. Do you think there is any shortage of water in the ocean?"

Shafik stares at John as if he has momentarily lost his mind. "Mister John, I can only see water. There is surely no shortage?"

"That is exactly what we will be chatting about tonight, Shafik: **a life of abundance**. And that is how our great Creator intended life to be. The ocean is full of water and living creatures. Rivers are filled with fresh water and fish. When you work the land, it is ready to give you a harvest. And we as God's children, can also live in such abundance, if we understand what life is truly about!"

John can see that a question is forming in Shafik's mind. The give-away is that little frown that starts appearing just between his eyes.

"Mister John, why then are there so many people on earth who live in incredible poverty?"

"That is a good question. And I do not have a complete answer for all poverty. But I think that if everyone understood what life is about and we lived accordingly, there would be less poverty and more abundant living. Maybe you will understand better when we have come to the end of tonight's visit."

The frown between Shafik's eyes has not let up.

"You see, Shafik, the Creator of everything we see around us is my God and Father. I am therefore one of His children here on earth. And when He sent His Son, Jesus, to earth to die for our sins, Jesus brought this message with Him: 'I came to give you life and life in abundance.' And this causes me to think differently about everything I do each day. Throughout the years I have come to realise how God truly blesses me with His abundance. This is one of the reasons why I want to share it with you. My heart is that you will also have and be part of this abundance, for the rest of your life!"

Shafik's words are barely audible above the crash of the waves against the bow. "That will be wonderful to live in such abundance."

The last sliver of sun disappears behind the horizontal line of the ocean and beautiful orange, pink and blue colours dance on the water and the sky for the last time that day. John slowly gets up to ask the captain to take the boat back closer to the mainland.

The captain switches on the engines and the lights on the yacht. With a soft hum, the yacht starts moving through the increasing darkness towards the lights of Cape Town. As the lights take on more individual forms, the captain switches off the engines and lowers the anchor for the night. They are just far enough off shore to still see the lights, but without being bothered by any of the sounds of the bustling city.

John pulls his deck chair closer to Shafik's while the cabin crew start preparing supper.

"Mister John?" Shafik looks over at his friend who now is only barely recognisable in the feint glow of the yacht lights. "This abundance you spoke about earlier. Does it relate only to money or is there more?"

"To me, abundance is much more than just money. When we talk about wealth, it relates to an abundance of valuable resources or material things. True wealth is the value of all assets owned by a country, a company or a person. It should be managed such that our children's children can benefit from it. Sometimes, when resources or material things are sold, the money can be mismanaged and be lost."

"Money is the system through which we buy or sell. The value of money is determined daily by the market. Now profit lies somewhere between wealth and money. Profit is when your money has worked for you and we mostly see it on the shares market, in bonds, and so on. Profit can be a big help to become wealthy because you can use it to buy assets to help you become rich."

"But, Mister John, how does one get profit to help you build wealth?"

"Rich people think differently about money compared to an ordinary person. Therefore, you must start thinking differently about wealth. While most people work for a salary, rich people think how they can use their money as a means to obtain more profit. They use other people's time and money in such a way that it becomes a lever with which large incomes can be generated. They handle risk in business constructively. All businesses have a measure of risk, but rich people just understand and calculate that risk better. And, should they make a mistake and experience large losses, they do not give up. They learn from their mistakes and that informs their decisions and actions going forward."

The sous chef arrives with their supper and they move over to the table. Between mouthfuls of the mouth-watering grilled tuna, Shafik asks, "You mentioned that rich people think differently about money. I also believe that profit is better than just getting a salary. But how does one get to that point that you have enough profit to become rich?"

John savours the delicious forkful of pulled pork before he answers.

"You will have to start your business somewhere, Shafik. Work fulltime at this new job you have just been appointed in and part time on your wealth. The day your part time business can financially support you, is the day you convert from your job to your passion. Does that make sense?"

"I think so. I will just have to make sure that it does not have a negative influence on my new job. Luckily I have a wise mentor who can give me advice." The smile around the corners of Shafik's mouth does not escape John's eyes.

As John reaches for the pepper, he makes a statement that slows down Shafik's chewing. "Your income is normally directly related to your personal development."

Shafik's fork hangs midair between his plate and his lips. "What do you mean, Mister John?"

"If you want to earn a billion rand, you need to grow into a billion-rand person. You need to develop in such a way that you are able to handle that billion so that you are ready to handle the second and so on."

Suddenly, a switch flicks on in Shafik's brain. "So, that is why we see each other so regularly. So that you can lead me to grow into that billion-rand person. And you can teach me because you have already developed to that level!?"

"Bingo!" John exclaims. "You must just remember that it is hard work. There will be pain: the pain of discipline and hard work, or the pain of regretting that you did not put in the hard work. Are you prepared to work hard, to start that business and to be financially free one day? Or are you going to sit back and let the government through social grants look after you in your old age?"

"No thank you! I have already decided that I want to start my own business, Mister John. I am just not sure what the best option is to begin with."

"I will help you choose, Shafik. But first, you will have to do some homework. Start investigating and listing ten businesses that you are interested in. The best options are those that you have a passion for. Then, write down the positive and negative aspects of each. From that list, choose a shortlist of three. Lastly, draw up an informal business plan for those three and try and determine the capital needed to start as well as possible profit margins. Bring that along for our next visit."

"Sure, that sounds like a great exercise!"

John greets his friend for the night and proceeds to the steps leading to the sleeping quarters. Halfway down, he calls to Shafik, "Won't you please have a look at the available apartments near your new work? Also, why you would choose the ones you list. Maybe we can have a look at when you will be able to afford a place of your own."

Shafik makes a mental note. He slowly takes a last deep breath of the ocean air and goes to bed. Tomorrow will be an early start. Try as he might, he cannot fall asleep quickly. Too many ideas are spinning in his head! Finally, and with the help of the easy sway of the yacht in the waves, he falls asleep.

Shafik's right arm slaps the bedside table to silence the alarm on his mobile phone. Through the haze, he sees that it is 5am. He jumps up, into his clothes and rushes onto the deck. John, laughing at the young man's sleepy features and spunky hairdo, hands him a steaming cup of coffee.

The fishing rods are ready, and the captain quickly shows him how to put on the bait. Shafik has had a few fishing experiences from the side of a river, but never in the open ocean. And the fish here obviously have different manners to river fish. But between the captain and John, Shafik quickly gets the hang of it. Soon, he has caught his third fish in a row.

With a twinkle in his now wide-awake eyes, he motions to John, "The ocean is truly filled with abundance today!" Both burst out laughing, knowing that there is a deeper truth to the words just uttered.

5. FARMING WITH FINANCES

A few weeks later, on a Friday afternoon, Shafik is picked up by a driver and they start their journey in the direction of Riebeeck West. Leaving the small town, they turn off at a farm gate. Shafik can see that the soil is very fertile. The vineyards look healthy and he notices the vegetable tunnels.

They arrive at the farmstead, and as Shafik open his door, he is met by the farm manager, who takes him to his room for the night. Then he accompanies the manager to view the tunnels and for a tour of the vineyards and he gets the opportunity to see how the produce is packaged.

Shafik is still marvelling at the variety, when the manager mentions that they also grow maize. They take a brisk walk to one of the maize fields. Shafik can smell the fresh earth that has recently been ploughed and the manager indicates that they plant the maize in phases to keep a continuous crop

Late afternoon, they return to the farm house. John walks out to greet them. Shafik proceeds to tell him what he has already seen.

"Are you up for one more walk, Shafik? I want to show you the poultry section ."

John shows Shafik the different divisions where they prepare chickens for the market, as well as the chicken coups where the eggs are produced. Everything is so organised, spotless and neat, which seems surprising to Shafik, given the township chickens he is used to.

Lastly, they walk over to where the eggs are packaged and labelled for the market. This must have involved a tremendous amount of planning and energy to get all the processes to run like a well-oiled machine.

Shafik cannot help but express his appreciation to the manager and John for having shown him around. With a deep laugh, John gives Shafik a gentle slap on the back. "It's a pleasure. And I can also hear your stomach grumbling, so let's head home for supper!"

The fire is already lit and echoes the colour of the sun that is just setting. With a cold drink in the hand, John and Shafik sit down and for a moment just marvel at the beauty around them.

"Mister, John," Shafik eagerly says, "I want to show you the apartments that I have listed."

Shafik extracts a neat set of notes with photos and prices and hands them over to John who carefully scans through the information and looks over at his friend.

"And, what do you think, Shafik?"

"What I did not know, is that most places require a month's rent as deposit in addition to the first month's rent. This is making it slightly more difficult to put in a bid immediately. But on the other hand, I don't want to lose the place," and Shafik leans over to show John his favourite flat.

"So, given your affirmation that you wrote, what would be the best way for you to secure this flat, Shafik?"

With this, Shafik removes another piece of paper from his folder and hands it over to John. It is his budget. "If I take my new salary, and save a bit more over the next three months, my debt will be paid off. Then I would be able to put down the deposit and the first month's rent. If this place is not available, I am sure there will be others in the same price range."

"That sounds like a brilliant strategy, Shafik! For this price, and given your new salary, you may even be able to negotiate with the owners to pay off the deposit over three months. Some property agencies are open for such a suggestion especially if they are keen to rent out a property. You will just need to show them proof of your previous salary slips with three months' worth of bank statements."

John lets the information sink in for a while. When he sees that Shafik seems to have grasped what he has suggested, he follows up with the next question.

"Have you had a chance to list some businesses you may want to get involved in, Shafik?"

Shafik's smile reveals that he had done just that. "I really enjoyed that exercise, Mister John," he says while taking out his note pad.

"It was very easy picking out the ten, but when I started sifting through them for the top three, I realised I needed money to get the business started effectively. If I must start with a zero budget, it is going to take a very long time to show a profit!"

John can hear the slight desperation in Shafik's voice. He carefully scrutinises the three choices Shafik has listed: a water-savings package for households and businesses; the planting of saffron on a small scale and the harvesting and selling thereof; and the establishment of a two-fold import/export business from Nigeria to South Africa: food from Nigeria to South Africa to cater for Nigerians in this country in exchange for solar panels for the provision of sustainable electricity for households and businesses who suffer frequent disruptions in Nigeria.

"This looks good, Shafik" John says deep in thought. "Maybe we should start working on the first business as a niche market for Cape Town given its water shortages. They are predicting more water shortages due to an influx of people into this Province. It also seems to me that this business would be less capital intensive to begin than the others. It is also something you can easily build after hours and you can use the internet to market and implement it. We can sharpen your business plan at a later stage to make it more effective. But I think you can start putting your systems in place to start marketing your product."

With that, John reaches across to Shafik and gives him the fourth box. The key inside is engraved with **"ABUNDANCE"**. Proudly, Shafik inserts it with the other three keys. His fingers inadvertently twirl around the keys; the principles engraved on them already starting to make a difference in his life.

"Would you mind making dinner for us on that fire tonight, Shafik?"

"Sure, Mister John! I do like making food. How do you like your meat?"

And with that, Shafik grabs the thongs and starts putting the meat on the grill.

Around the dinner table, Shafik takes the opportunity to ask more questions about the farm and all the different businesses he saw that afternoon. It is evident that farming is close to John's heart and he elaborates in detail how the different sections started out and how he has been able to ensure good and growing profit margins on each.

After dinner, with their chairs pulled closer to the fire, John looks over to Shafik.

"Do you know why I brought you out to the farm, Shafik?"

"Mister John, honestly? I don't have a clue. All I know is that this place is beautiful and can teach me a great deal about farming. In fact, I think my entrepreneurial heart is turning into a farming heart!"

John chuckles. "That is good to hear, Shafik! To be truly successful in life, one must be able to treat your finances like a farmer. Do you remember when you walked in the maize field this afternoon?"

Shafik nods.

"The best seed must be planted in the right soil at the right time with enough water. Then you enter a waiting period while the seed germinates, grows, and bears fruit before you can harvest. Does that make sense?"

"Yes, Mister John. But what does that have to do with success?" Shafik asks with interest.

"Let me share with you a secret few people understand, Shafik. Sowing is a principle that our Creator has built into creation. The more you sow, the more you reap. God is the Giver of all good things in abundance. He has created nature to be able to give: clouds give rain, rivers give water, the sun gives light and plants give us oxygen and food. Because we were created in the image of God, He wants us also to be people who will be spontaneous in our giving. And the more we give Him the honour, the more He gives back to us. In fact, we are therefore farmers on God's farm, with the ability to sow throughout our time on earth. And when we discover how to hear God's voice and we give when He says so, then eternal streams of provision open up into our lives. Those who grasp this, become rich by sowing here on earth."

Shafik has listened so intently, that he has forgotten to blink. His eyes start watering. He blinks a few times quickly while he tries to formulate a response to what he has just heard.

"What you have just said, Mister John, I have never heard

before. How on earth do I sow practically in my life and in my business?"

John shifts around in his chair until he reaches a place of comfort. He then takes a sip of his coffee.

"Maybe I should tell you where I am coming from, before I answer your question. I believe that those who sow a little, will only reap a little. Those who sow abundantly, will reap abundantly. The Bible says in Luke 6:38: *Give, and it shall be given unto you; good measure, pressed down, and shaken together, and running over, shall men give into your bosom. For with the same measure that ye mete withal it shall be measured to you again.*"

"When I hear the Holy Spirit talking to me, then I give with a wide, open hand and with overflowing joy in my heart. Sometimes I see how God rewards me with a double portion, more than what I have given away. Other times, it is like the farmer who has planted the seeds and has to wait a season before he can harvest. The most important question to ask yourself: do you have seed in the ground? If the farmer has not sown, he cannot expect a harvest."

"That sounds logical, Mister John" Shafik replies while he sits trying to make sure that he remembers all that John is teaching him.

"To answer your question, Shafik: there are three ways in which I normally give. I give a tenth of all my income for the work of the Lord. This is a Biblical principle and even non-believers who give their money to charities, will tell you how their income just keeps growing. In the Old Testament of the Bible, Malachi 3:10 promises us that God will open the windows of heaven and provide for me when I give my tenth. He promises that He will ensure that my enemy does not harm me. There is a supernatural blessing linked to giving your tenth."

John can sense he has Shafik's entire focus and concentration.

"The second way, is when I hear God's voice and He shows me where to sow. Many times, when I sow in this manner, I will name that seed and ask God to bless it."

Shafik's frown is back and he asks, "What do you mean by naming your seed?"

"We never give to receive anything back. We sow out of thankfulness and obedience. But because I know that seed always offers a harvest, I expect God to provide that harvest for me. And, should there be areas where I need God's blessing, then I will tell Him about it."

John can see that Shafik still does not grasp what this way of giving means.

"I'll give you an example, Shafik. Let's say I give an old widow a month's worth of groceries, then I will christen this seed 'provision for my children'. I will then ask God, 'Lord, as I am now giving in obedience to this widow, will You please provide for my children?'"

"Oh, now I understand," says Shafik.

"Sowing can really be a great adventure in your life, Shafik! My wife and I do something we call 'God's purse'. We buy cheap purses at the local Chinese shop. Then we wait upon the Lord to hear how much money He wants us to put inside the purse. That money, we dedicate to God and we do not touch it. When we meet the person, God intended the money for, we give that purse and explain what God has placed on our hearts. The joy and thankfulness on the person's face when he or she realises that the Creator of heaven and earth has sent supernatural provision for them, is priceless!"

It is slowly dawning on Shafik that John may have been chosen to get involved in his life because that same Creator has placed it on John's heart. Something about this God of John is stirring his heart. Shafik feels like he is losing control and quickly parks the thought.

"Are there more ways in which you sow, Mister John?"

"Yes, there is one more way that I have not shared with many people. I give away the first fruits of my harvest."

"Do you mean your maize or grape harvest?"

John smiles. "Something like that, Shafik. Every time I receive a new stream of income or if there is an increase in my normal income, I give that first part in its entirety to the Lord. From the next month onwards, I give a tenth of my new income back to the Lord. And you can see how good Father God has been to me. He truly blesses everything I start under His guidance."

"Will you help me to become a farmer on God's farm, Mister John?" Shafik asks this truthfully. "I...I can see that this is working in your life."

"I will gladly help you, Shafik. But there is one more principle that I strongly believe in as a farmer and that deals with digging wells. Abraham in the Bible, farmed in an arid land with sheep and cattle. He dug all over the place to ensure that his animals had access to water. He later moved to a land with more resources. But when his son, Isaac, started farming in the same dry area where his father used to farm, he re-opened all the wells his father had dug. He also dug more wells."

"This story from the Bible has taught me that one should always go and dig again where there once was water. If a business has worked for a person in a certain way, it may work for me: I must just go and re-open that well for fresh water. But I should also search for direction from God what new wells I have to go and dig. That is like the top three businesses you have listed for tonight. All three sounds like new wells and maybe the Lord wants to give you strong flowing water through them. You just have to go and dig, even if it is hard work!"

"Mister John, that sure is a powerful image you have given me. I have never been afraid of hard work, and I would want to start digging on my first well as soon as possible!"

John is satisfied that Shafik is really listening to what he is trying to teach him.

"Shafik, maybe for our next session you can jot down how you as a farmer will sow in the business world and how you will dig those wells to find fresh water?"

"That sounds like a great challenge, Mister John!"

And with that, the evening draws to a close. The last embers still give a red shimmer now and then. Tomorrow, Shafik will get the chance to drive a tractor and plant some seeds: one step closer to a harvest.

6. BRILLIANT MANAGERS

It is 09:00 on Saturday morning, three weeks after their farm excursion. It is quiet in the office block where John has his work space. Shafik hands over his notes where he has set out how he intends farming in the business world:

- He has shown how he can sow 10% of his income every month, but above and beyond that, he also wants to sow where God directs him - especially to those who are having a tough time.
- And he plans to sow his first fruits, but he acknowledges to John that he is still uncertain about how exactly this works.
- He will start investigating the three businesses on his list to see whether other people have started similar businesses and how they have run such enterprises. Then he would not have to make the same mistakes they have made.
- He also wants to 'dig wells' close to John to ensure that he can tap into his wisdom and experience.

John silently sits and watches Shafik as his hands talk along while he gives more detail on the points he had written down. He seamlessly flows over into telling John about his new job and how he is utterly enjoying the new challenge. At last, he pulls out two sets of keys: one of a vehicle and the other to his new apartment!

John cannot contain himself, jumps up and gives Shafik a great big bear hug! "Well done, Shafik! I am so glad!"

And with that, John hands over the fifth golden key to success to Shafik. Shafik rubs his finger over the engraving: **"SOW"**.

"Shafik, I would like you to spend an hour or two with my general manager of imports and exports. I am convinced you will learn a lot in your session with Mr Davids."

"Thanks, Mister John! But, uhm..." Shafik clears his throat and suddenly seems uneasy.

"What is it, Shafik? Did something happen?"

"I...I have been thinking about this a long time, Mister John. I don't really know how to ask you. Will you....will you help me to get to know God better? Maybe I can also hear His voice? And serve Him like you do?"

"Phew, Shafik!" says John with a huge sigh of relief. "For a moment, I really thought something terrible has happened! Of course, I will help you get to know God!"

And John proceeds to tell Shafik how much God loves him, and that Jesus was sent to earth to die for his sin because he wanted to save Shafik! All he has to do is to repent of his sins and to ask God for forgiveness. Then he can ask Jesus to become his personal Saviour and Redeemer!

Shafik carefully sits down. There is a light blush on his cheeks. "Mister John?" he hesitantly asks. "I have never really prayed. Would you mind praying and then I can repeat what you said, please?"

John nods and asks Shafik to repeat after him: "Jesus, I am sorry about all my sins. Please forgive me? I accept you as my personal Saviour. Amen."

When John opens his eyes, he sees tears streaming down Shafik's face. John pulls him close and the silence that surrounds them seems different to other times; Godly. When Shafik has regained his composure, John puts his hands on Shafik's shoulders and looks him in the eye.

"Shafik, will you accept me as your father in the faith?"

Shafik cannot control his tears. He rushes back into John's arms. Finally, he has someone that he can look up to as a father. Even

John is struggling to hold back his tears. Now, he has a son.

"So, what does a new Christian do, Mister John?" Shafik's smile is back and he brushes the last trace of tears from his cheeks.

"Well, you can start by reading your Bible and praying. Praying is just you talking to God, about anything at any time. And then, if you want, you come and join our Thursday care-group. There you will grow and learn about your new King."

While he is still speaking, John gets up and takes his own Bible with its brown leather cover from the shelf. "Start reading the Book of John. From today onwards, this is your Bible." John takes a pen and writes the date and time Shafik accepted Jesus Christ and he ends off with:

To my son, Shafik.
With love,
Your spiritual father,
John.

Shafik takes the Bible and presses it against his heart. He picks up his backpack and carefully slides the Bible inside. It is time for him to meet the general manager.

Mr Davids is a senior man and it seems as if he could be close to retirement. He warmly greets Shafik and invites him into his office. He starts showing Shafik the finer detail of their very diverse business that he has been involved in for 31 years. Shafik notices how loyal Mr Davids is towards John as executive director and the pride he has for the company.

After two hours, Shafik stretches his hand out to Mr Davids to say goodbye. As a parting thought, Shafik asks whether he may at some stage, come and discuss the costs of exporting to Nigeria. Mr Davids hands him his business card and invites him to come by any time.

Shafik's smile is wrapped around his head as he walks back into John's office.

"Well, it looks like you had a good time, Shafik?"

"Mister John! This has truly been one of the most memorable in my life. The import and export business really fascinates me and Mr Davids is a wonderful teacher! I feel strongly that my 'third' business might happen first!"

John has a good laugh with Shafik and he pours them both a fresh cup of coffee.

"Shafik, I am truly thankful about your spiritual decision this morning. It just makes it so much easier to have a chat about our next topic: brilliant managers or stewards."

"The Greek word in the Bible for "steward" is *'oikonomos'*. It translates into 'managing a household'. In Biblical times, the manager of a household held all the responsibility including cleaning the house, ensuring there is sufficient food, that all the workers gave their best effort and to ensure that there is a financial budget. Stewardship is therefore to responsibly manage everything that has been placed in your care."

"When God created Adam and Eve, He appointed them over everything on earth. In Psalm 24:1, it says that the entire cosmos belongs to God. When you and I understand that in business, we have been appointed by God as managers or stewards of His property, it changes the way we deal with His property."

Shafik nods. "That sounds like a big responsibility, Mister John!"

"Yes, Shafik. We must manage God's resources and finances well to ensure God, as our Chief Executive Officer, is happy. And that includes determining the best strategy and keeping at it continuously. Stewardship, in the end, becomes a way of life and is not just limited to the business world. If God calls you today to be a steward of His household on earth, would you be up for it, Shafik?"

Shafik's fingers play with the pages of his note pad while he thinks it over. "It is really such a big responsibility. But after this morning, and all that He has forgiven me for, it is all I want to do, Mister John!"

"That is good news, Shafik. This brings us to a pivotal aspect of being a manager: how we manage our time. Many people spend their time on urgent things that are happening around them instead of focusing on the important things we were called for."

John takes a moment, and Shafik takes the gap to share his experience.

"I must admit that I fell into this trap yesterday. I was sidetracked by urgent phone calls and emails while the manager was waiting for an important strategy I was supposed to present to him about our apple business in Grabouw. I knew the strategy was vitally important, yet I spent my time unnecessarily on what I thought was the urgent stuff."

"Exactly, Shafik," John affirms. "One can always call a client back and apologise for not being able to answer his call immediately. They may even have more respect for you because you phoned back on the same day. If we do not plan our lives well and stick to it, we can easily be led by someone else's plans. This can bring about a lot of frustration. But the choice remains ours," John's words echoes in Shafik's ears.

"Would you advise me to attend a course on time management, Mister John?"

"I will let you know when I hear about such a course. In the meantime, there are easy-read books on the subject. And of course, you can ask this old man for some tips!" John says with a smile in his voice.

"Sure, 'old man'!" Shafik bursts out laughing for this title John has given himself. He has noticed that John is very punctual and that he delegates work to his secretary. He actively plans his day so that he spends time on the important things. Shafik has never seen John in a hurry or stressed out about an issue. It is evident that John is manageing his schedule and not the other way round.

Shafik gets pulled out of his thought-pool by John's question.

"Shafik, do you see yourself as a leader?"

"Mister John, I am a 23-year-old man with a poverty-stricken past who has just started a brand new job in a brand new field. I would like to think that one day I can become a strong leader, but now, I see myself only as an apprentice...under your guidance of course."

"That is a brilliant answer, Shafik!" John is impressed with Shafik's sober view of himself. "Any person can be a leader. Studies have shown that even the least of us get a chance to influence at least 10,000 people in our life time - positively or negatively. Given our role as managers on earth, it should always be our aim to impart a positive influence on people's thoughts, beliefs and deeds."

Shafik seems thankful. "If I measure myself against that, then I am a leader; albeit at the start of the leadership journey."

John continues. "People follow a leader because they believe in him. That is why leaders must live with integrity so that people would want to follow them. You need to live what you speak. Be optimistic and work with a vision for the future. People want to know that, where they are heading to under your leadership, is better than where they are now. Care for people, not just for what you can gain from them. Build a strong leadership team around you and enhance their leadership. Encourage them to raise up leaders."

"That seems like a mouthful, Mister John, but I want to start and have to start somewhere!"

"It takes a leader to equip other leaders, Shafik. King David in the Bible had 400 brave men around him whom he equipped to lead. Five of those men killed giants, but not before David killed the first giant. We teach others that which we know, but in fact we are reproducing who we are."

John's eyes suddenly seem on fire to Shafik.

"With everything in me I want to encourage you, Shafik: be a leader who trains eagles - leaders with great vision; leaders who can soar high above the others and who are not scared of the storm. Leaders who can change the world!"

Shafik feels goose-flesh all over his body. John's enthusiasm is electric!

"What do I do to become a leader like that, Mister John? What do I read?"

"There are many good books about leadership, Shafik. Two that really helped me were John Maxwell's 'The Irrefutable Laws of Leadership' and 'The Five Levels of Leadership'. Don't try and read the books in one session. There are so many truths in it, that you will have to take time to think it over and work at it, before moving on to the next part. Most leaders have a few books that they always go back to."

John gives Shafik a chance to finish writing down the names of the books he recommended.

"Great leaders change atmospheres where they move. I believe you have the potential to be a great leader, Shafik. Remember, it will be a process. Leadership is formed daily; not in a day."

Shafik nods.

"This means a lot to me, Mister John. I mean...your belief in me."

John smiles at Shafik and warmly says, "It's is my pleasure. For next time, won't you please write down what you believe the ideal qualities of a steward or manager should be?"

Shafik assures John that it will be done and starts packing away his notepad and pen. John watches him as he neatly places everything in his backpack.

"Before you run off, I have one more story to tell." Shafik sinks back into the comfortable chair.

"In a faraway place, there was a great lake high in the mountains with an almost infinite flow of water. From the lake, three rivers formed, the flow of each which could be controlled by means of a sluice- gate. At the foot of the mountain, a farmer, who believed that one could never have enough water, made his home next to one of the rivers. He built a dam to redirect water from the river so that he would always have a supply of water.

Next to the second river lived a woman who believed that there would always be enough water for her needs. She took from the river only that which she needed. The rest of the water, flowed passed her house and fed the people downstream.

The farmer living next to the third river was a personal friend of the owner of the big lake. He was therefore not concerned with storing up water, as he knew the capacity of the lake and that the owner wanted those people downstream to have sufficient water at all times.

This farmer therefore made innovative plans to direct the water to as many people as possible who were not located next to the river. Every year, he would dig canals to places that had never had rivers running passed them. He would buy the equipment to dig the canals and even made them available to those people who were the beneficiaries of the canals, to help dig canals for their neighbours."

"To which of the three rivers, do you think, Shafik, did the owner of the lake allocate the most water every day?"

Shafik takes a moment to recall the three options. "I guess the third river, Mister John? That guy was really concerned about sharing what he had with others."

"You're right, Shafik. This is why we were called as stewards of God's household: so that those around us can have access to what we have received." And with that, John gets up from his chair, stretches out his hand, and greets his friend Shafik.

With his mind overflowing with information and a new destiny in Christ Jesus, Shafik swings his backpack onto his shoulders and walks to his vehicle.

A great sense of peace rests upon him. Maybe he will be someone to dig canals to God's people. To feed them what flows through him...

7. WILL YOU JUMP?

Shafik spots the sign board to the Durbanville Flying Club and takes a right turn onto the gravel road. He wonders what this day's session with John will involve.

As he pulls up to the club house, he sees John standing at the entrance. Shafik and John exchange pleasantries and, as they sit down at a table, Shafik hands over his list of qualities that a steward or manager should possess. As John reads through the list, he nods in agreement.

"Well said, Shafik!" John reaches into his shirt pocket and hands over the sixth key. In gold Shafik reads the engraving: **MANAGERS**.

"If I have summed you up correctly, Shafik, you do like adventure? Are you ready for another big one?"

Shafik looks around and with hesitation, he says, "Yes, I think I am, but surely I should know what I am letting myself in for?"

John chuckles."I have taken the liberty of buying us each a jump."

Shafik's frown is back. He did not know that one could buy a jump? "What do you mean you bought a jump, Mister John?"

"We are going to sky dive, Shafik!"

Shafik's brown complexion turns pale and a slight sweat breaks out just above his eye brows. He most definitely was not expecting this.

"Is someone going to teach me? Or are we just expected to

jump out of the plane? What if I make a mistake? I thought one has to do a course first?"

John laughs at the barrage of questions pouring out of Shafik's nervous body. "Don't worry Shafik. I have organised with an instructor to walk us through the steps. He will also do your first jump in tandem with you."

John and Shafik leave their valuables in the safe at the club house. They walk over to the hangar where the instructor welcomes them. On the big screen, the instructor runs through what will happen from the moment they leave the ground until they land safely back on mother earth. In the hanger, they practice a few jumps and are taught how to land correctly.

Too soon to Shafik's liking, it is time to board the plane. The engine noise makes it almost impossible to talk and as the aircraft picks up speed, Shafik's heart races. Some part is excitement but mostly he fears the unknown. Who would have thought the guy living in a tin hut a few months ago, would now jump out of an airplane?

John is an old hand when it comes to sky diving. As soon as they reach the correct height, John reaches past Shafik to open the door. He gives Shafik a thumbs-up signal to show him it's time to stand up and walk towards the opening. Quick as lighting, and before Shafik can get up, John jumps out of the plane. Shafik rushes to the door, just in time to see John's parachute opening.

By this time, the instructor screams above the engine noise and whipping wind that it is their turn. With his fingers, the instructor counts down from three and without doing much, Shafik's body leaves the plane.

The first few seconds of free fall feels like an eternity. Shafik feels his cheeks being pulled back and in his mind, he can just imagine what his flapping cheeks look like! But, just as quickly, both he and the instructor are pulled back when the parachute finally opens. Their speed reduces drastically and Shafik allows himself to look to the ground. Everything looks so small! He feels strangely at peace and very happy, considering he is floating thousands of feet above earth.

With a deft turn of the parachute, Shafik and the instructor land safely on the spot that was agreed upon at the start. It is a soft landing and both manage to stay on their feet. They clip themselves free, and while Shafik is still busy with his last clip, John pounces on him with a jubilant, "You did it!".

Back at the club house with a cappuccino in hand, John says, "To be an entrepreneur, is like taking your first sky dive. It remains a big risk, but a calculated one. You must always be convinced that there are enough positive aspects that count in your favour, before you take the risk."

Shafik could not have had a better practical explanation than having just jumped out of an aeroplane.

"Shafik, we must move on from the 'old type economy' we grew up with. Things like a secure income, great employment benefits and building a pension, will slowly but surely start disappearing. It is now time for a new generation of entrepreneurs to stand up."

"That is all well and good, Mister John, but what is an entrepreneur?"

"Shafik, entrepreneurs are those people who see opportunity, take it and turn it into a business to fulfil their dreams. A true entrepreneur never fails at business. The perceived failure is turned into a learning experience which he or she then uses the next time they take a risk. Does this resonate with you?"

Shafik is stunned. "When I was little, I was always taking chances, to my mother's frustration! Risk somehow has never scared me, though this jump came close!" Both burst out laughing.

John reaches into his brief case and places two books on the table. Shafik struggles to pronounce the author's name, and John helps him.

"Robert T Kiyosaki wrote two books that I can highly recommend: Cash Flow Quadrant and Midas Touch. The last one he wrote with Donald J Trump. Have you read any of these, Shafik?"

"No, I have never heard of these books."

"Basically, there are four types of people. Employees who never really become wealthy; small business owners working for themselves who are better off than the employees working for them; big business owners who are very wealthy and have more than 500 people in their employment; and lastly, investors who have let other people and their money work for them. The last group is also the only group that can truly live financially free lives."

John gives Shafik a moment to digest the four types of people. "Which one of these would you like to be, Shafik?"

"Surely, I would like to fall into the last category, Mister John? For now, I am an employee, who is looking to move over to the small business category. In a few years, I want to be a big business owner. But I already now want to start investing!"

John beams. "That is a great answer, Shafik! I still believe with my whole heart that you are well on your way to be successful."

John picks up the 'Midas Touch' book and holds it in the air. "In this book, the author uses the five fingers on a hand to describe the attributes of an entrepreneur. The thumb represents strong character. It is not always moonshine and roses in business. You have to be able to handle pressure, stress and fear. Someone once said that *'Life is like a grindstone. Whether it grinds you down or polishes you up, depends on what you are made of.'"*

The second finger represents focus to keep going until you are successful. The middle finger represents branding. A great brand starts in the heart of an entrepreneur and it touches the heart of the end-user. You have to ensure that your brand is the best and that it can be marketed worldwide. The ring finger represents relationships. That is the most important finger as you will need to build relationships with those in business with you. It may also unlock new opportunities for you. Lastly, the little finger represents the small things that count: speed, quality and integrity. The things that will give you the competitive edge."

"It sounds like I have some reading and learning to do, Mister John!"

"Yes, Shafik, and for next time, you can bring me a summary of one of these books for our discussion."

Shafik carefully places the books in his backpack.

The next question hits Shafik when he sits down in the chair..

"What are your thoughts on different streams of income, Shafik?"

"I think it is important to diversify if you want to become rich, Mister John. My only problem is that I don't know exactly how to do it."

John takes a handful of peanuts from the bowl on the table. "You're correct. In today's world, it is a risk to have only a single stream of income. To protect your income, you need a range of income sources. That is what you saw on my farm. When one department suffers a blow, the other departments can help carry it."

"But, how and where does one start?" Shafik asks with his famous frown back between his eyes.

"In the first place, you need a stable monthly income. That can be your current job or business, but it must be able to sustain you for the next year while you are building your other income stream. If possible, it is best to build one income stream at a time and not get greedy and build three or four. This way you can make sure that you can build a strong business."

"Invest in expertise, someone like a business coach. The little you spend for such expertise, can save you a lot in future. Make sure you know exactly what you want to do: you are looking for a niche market with a need that your product or service can fulfil. There are also administrative considerations like registering your business correctly, having a proper budget and bookkeeping system, and opening a bank account. Your marketing must be done well and you need to plan when you want to start implementing your business. Be ready to work hard and to endure as it will take time for the business to be established. Some people say that it takes 1000 days to really solidify your business."

Shafik swallows hard. That was another mouthful and somewhere deep inside he feels like he is standing on the edge of a cliff, and that the slightest wind will push him into despair. But his sense of adventure and willingness to take risks, quickly helps dissolve that feeling that wants to overwhelm him.

"Yes, Mister John," Shafik bravely answers. "This helps a lot!"

"If you're not busy, Shafik, I would like you to join my family for the long weekend. We are going to row on a portion of the Orange River. You are my guest and there is no charge."

Shafik does not even have to look at the calendar on his mobile phone. "That sounds great, Mister John!"

"Wonderful, Shafik! I will email you what you need to take along!"

And so, Shafik leaves his adventurous afternoon with even

8. ENJOY LIFE!

more knowledge and a greater desire to learn.
Shafik struggles to open the vehicle door. There is nothing wrong with the key, it is just his excitement to get home and grab his weekend bag that is causing him to fumble.

When the phone rings in his apartment, he knows his lift has arrived, and he runs down the stairs. John's four-wheel vehicle with a trailer is waiting outside. John packs Shafik's bag and laptop safely in the back.

Inside, Shafik greets John's wife, Charmaine, and their eighteen-year-old daughter, Michaela. Both women agree to sit in the back so that John and Shafik can talk business in front. They have barely turned onto the national road, when the first round of sandwiches is handed out.

"I can see this is going to be a very good weekend if this is the way it starts!" Shafik jokingly says. Everyone bursts out laughing and there is a warm and excited atmosphere in the vehicle.

Shafik asks Michaela to pass him his laptop bag and removes one of the latest books John lent him. John directs Shafik to place it in the holder underneath the arm rest. Shafik struggles to insert the book, and when he reaches down to see what is obstructing his way, he finds a little box.

John looks over and smilingly says, "Open it, Shafik!"

Shafik takes out the seventh key engraved with **'ENTREPRENEUR'** and adds it to the other six keys. For a while they both just enjoy the scenery and relaxed atmosphere.

Out of the blue John makes a statement, "It is important that your outside reflects accurately what is happening on your inside."

Shafik and his frown looks over at John. "I have no idea what you mean. It is after all a Friday afternoon, Mister John and I think my brain has switched off!"

John smiles. "I am talking about three-dimensional health. Each of us are made up of three parts: body, soul and spirit. We must ensure that we work at all three areas for optimum health. Then your outside will reflect your inside. Most people choose one area to excel in, like the body. They will exercise ferociously, but will not be balanced as they have neglected the other two parts."

Shafik ponders a while. "But what is the difference between soul and spirit? Is it not the same thing, Mister John?"

Shafik can hear Michaela chuckle at him addressing her father as 'Mister John'.

"Your soul, Shafik, is your basic intellect, your emotions and will. But your spirit is that part of you that has to do with eternity. The day you were saved, your spirit was renewed. But there are many things in your soul that still require work. Things that we should work on daily."

"So, you are saying that we can exercise our souls just as much as our bodies?"

"Something like that, Shafik!"

Shafik starts thinking about the condition of his own body. "I have a relatively healthy body which I exercise regularly. But I do have a sweet tooth and I drink too much Coke. I definitely need to work on those!"

"That's true. What we put in our mouths not only affects our body, but also the workings of our brain. And how much do you sleep, Shafik?"

"Well, I'm actually a morning person and always up early. In the last few months however, and with the pressure of my new job, I do not get to bed as early as I would like to. My coach also wants a report every time we visit," Shafik adds with a twinkle in his eye. "In total, I would therefore say that I sleep between five and six hours a night, Mister John. Is that enough?"

"It may differ from person to person, but the really smart guys tell us that we need between seven and eight hours sleep per night. Every hour you get into bed before 12, is worth almost as much as two hours after 12. You need enough sleep in your 'deep sleep phase' to be able to dream. During the time we sleep, the body has a chance to rejuvenate itself. That is why doctors recommend sleep therapy for those who have burnt out or are dealing with depression. Sleep also helps us to process the day's events. And while we sleep, our brain produces new brain cells!"

"Okay, Mister John, I get it that we can look after our bodies. So, when it comes to our spirit, we can exercise it by reading the Bible and praying; or being among people of the same faith?" Shafik suggests.

"Spot on, Shafik!"

"But what do I do about my soul? To which gym can I take it?" Shafik asks.

"This is one of the most important areas that people neglect. The sessions we do, help us intellectually to learn new things and to challenge one another. That is why I continuously suggest new reading material to you. You can also do self-study in any field that interests you to increase your general knowledge. Those day-time soapies on television do not necessarily help!" John teases Shafik.

"Shafik, do you remember when we talked about the brain and how those new neurons are formed from positive thoughts that we speak out loud? That helps to keep our emotions healthy. Throughout my years, I have consciously cut out people who keep on slandering others, and speak negatively. I still love them, but they do not form part of my circle of friends."

Shafik is quiet for a few moments.

"It must have been hard to cut out those people, Mister John. How did you do it? I work with some of them!"

"Firstly, Shafik, we must understand how people's thought processes work and then we must deal with it. Some people live as though they are garbage collector trucks. They pick up negative talk or dirty thoughts and put them in their truck. Then they proceed to look for people who will either validate whatever negative or dirty words they speak, or on which they can dump their negativity. In love, I choose not to allow this in my life. I have learnt to either redirect the conversation or to walk away. If they take offence, it is their choice. But because I do it in love, I have found that most people will respect my decision. You may even be able to help those people to listen to their own words and change their way of speaking. Does that make sense, Shafik?"

"Sure, Mister John. It does seem that you have had lots of practice!"

"The best type of exercise for our emotions are found in Romans 12:1-2 in the Bible. It challenges us to go through a process of change or metamorphosis from pupae to butterflies. We must totally renew our thoughts. And that takes patience and perseverance."

"You do know that you will have to teach me how to do that, Mister John?!"

"The more you read the Bible, the more you will become aware of how God wants you to live. As you have learnt, with repeating positive thoughts, if we don't water the negative thoughts our old thought patterns die off and the new ones get stronger and stronger. In this way, we can renew our thoughts and become completely new. We become more and more like God in our emotions, will and thoughts."

Shafik acknowledges that he did not really understand why he needed to read his Bible every day. Now it makes more sense.

"I will leave you with one last thought before we go into 'weekend mode', Shafik. We need to learn to have fun, to build in adventure and to laugh. Laughing is extremely good exercise for our brains. It releases endorphins or 'feel good' hormones that help your body spontaneously fight disease. Positive and happy people have far fewer appointments with the doctor because their spirit, soul and body are in harmony."

Shafik shakes his head in disbelief. "Is that really true, Mister John?"

"Yes, it is. I believe that with each work assignment, to ensure that there is a little bit of adventure. The last time I went to work in Mombasa, Kenya, I made sure that I regularly went for a walk on the beach. We also made time to go snorkeling among the reefs. We also had lots of laughs at the antics of our travelling companions, especially the one who was given an oversize pair of flip flops to snorkel with!" John remembers with a smile.

"Is there anything you want me to prepare for the next meeting, Mister John?" Shafik asks, seeing that their formal meeting was drawing to a close.

John thinks a moment and then asks Shafik to prepare a few notes on how he was going to maintain his three-dimensional health for the rest of his life.

Seven hours later, at 22:00, they stop at the border post with Namibia and move swiftly through. They drive on and take the turn-off to the Amanzi Trails River Camp. The guard at the gate hands them their keys and in the headlights, Shafik notices the green grass and big trees.

John's family works like a well-oiled machine and soon all the necessities have been packed out in their self-catering chalet. Just before midnight, everyone is in bed.

At five o'clock the next morning, John gets everyone up like a drill sergeant and makes sure they have coffee and something to eat. They need to report to the tour guides with their rucksacks, sleeping bags and three days' food. The tour guide gives them a quick overview of the do's and don'ts on the river and they start packing their canoes.

It is Shafik's first time in a canoe, and he is hesitant about the canoe's ability to keep him out of the water, given the loaded 25 litre drums, and all their other equipment. Luckily, there are two guides who will go with them and they seem to be experts in the water.

The boats slip quietly into the water and the sun is already baking out of the Namibian sky. Downstream paddling seems easy enough to Shafik and he gets an opportunity to stare in amazement at the rock formations. He manages to stay in the boat while navigating the first few rapids and finds some comfort in the fact that they all have to wear life jackets.

Too soon the day draws to an end and it's time to set up camp. Tents shoot up like mushrooms and sleeping bags are rolled out while the guides make a fire for coffee and supper. John looks around the camp and can see his team is wasted but happy. The sun and fun had the last say and everyone gets to bed early.

The next morning, Shafik is proud of the fact that he can help to get the canoes ready. Everything seems much easier this morning and the team spends another fun-filled day on the river. Deep in his heart, Shafik has decided that he will make a point of going on an adventurous holiday with his friends and family at least once a year.

After three days of rowing, camping and having fun, they spend their last night alongside the Orange River. Curled up in his sleeping bag after supper, Shafik feels an overwhelming sense of thankfulness towards John, Charmaine and Michaela. He knows that it was a divine connection orchestrated by God. He would not mind journeying the rest of his life with these three people.

Every second thought is interrupted with Michaela's face. Her shiny black hair and sun-tanned skin; her beautiful smile and bubbly personality. But she is John's daughter and moves in other social circles than Shafik does. He parks the thought, knowing that he does not want to do anything to spoil his friendship with this family; especially not his fast-growing feelings for this dark-haired beauty. And with that, Shafik falls asleep.

At 06:00 the next morning, the vehicle taking the team back to camp, has been packed and is ready to go. Things move quickly once they are back at camp and before 9am, John, his family and Shafik are on their way to the border post.

Once cleared and back on the road to Cape Town, John is ready with his first discussion point.

"Let's talk about relationships, Shafik!" Shafik's heart misses a beat and he wonders whether John has been reading his thoughts. He was thinking about Michaela again. Shafik sees out of the corner of his eye that the two ladies are leaning forward, wanting to take part in this conversation.

John notices it too and smiles at his wife in the rear-view mirror before he continues. "Great relationships are vital for success in your life. Through relationships, we are exposed to the greatest experiences, but also the deepest pain. It all depends how we handle our relationships with others."

Shafik nods. "But are you only referring to relationships between family members, or also relationships at work, Mister John?"
"Shafik, I am referring to all types of relationships. And therefore, we need to develop our interpersonal skills. Successful people have great relationships in their family setup and are able to deal with all people; be it the difficult or the uncomplicated ones."

"To have great relationships with nice people, is not difficult. But you know, there are some interesting personalities that just get to me" Shafik reacts.

John nods in acknowledgement. "I see relationships as a garden. You can have a messy garden or a manicured one that has been looked after. It all depends whether you are willing to work in the garden, mow the lawn, prune the trees, and get rid of the alien plants wanting to take over. If not, that garden will go to waste. Someone once said that you should always make an effort to put in time and imagination to let any relationship grow."

"Gmp," Shafik snorts with a little bit of disgust. "There are some relationships where I would need to use a lot of imagination! And what does that mean in any event?"

"I think the person was just trying to say that you cannot do the same thing in every relationship. Every person is different and therefore you need to have a different approach with each person. You need to think creatively and bring in a bit of adventure, especially in your relationships with your life partner and your family, Shafik."

Shafik looks down at his hands, embarrassed that he was so flippant about 'imagination'.

"I will give you an example," Charmaine says, trying to talk away the evident embarrassment. "You can bring your wife breakfast in bed, buy her flowers and expensive perfume, and take her out to dinners!"

"Or take her out on a sunset boat cruise, walk with her on the beach or take her on a dream holiday to Mauritius!" pips Michaela.

John just shakes his head. "You see, Shafik, that is why we need to discuss business out of ear shot of the ladies. Can you see how many fresh, new problems I have just created for myself!?" They all burst out laughing at John's seemingly self-imposed misfortunes.

"Ah, Dad! You promised to still take us to Mauritius this year. Just think about the many creative inspirations you will find on that island to build relationships!" Michaela adds with a laugh and a pleading note in her voice.

"I hear you, Michaela, but maybe we can wait a bit to build the expensive part of our relationship!" John says smilingly while he watches his daughter sit back in her seat, grinning from ear to ear and satisfied that she could contribute to the conversation.

"Shafik, you are a leader. And you will work with people the rest of your life, whether it is at work, in your social life or in your family. It will not always be easy. My suggestion is that you start working now already, as a young man, to learn how to build relationships with all types of people. See if you can find John Maxwell's book 'Be a People Person'. I have learned many valuable lessons from it and refer to it regularly to sharpen my skills."

"Okay, Mister John. I get it: I need to spend time in the 'relationship' garden and the ladies certainly helped me understand the imagination part. But are you talking about the quality of the time spent or the quantity?"

John's mouth is still forming the first word, when Charmaine chips in. "When it comes to your life partner and your family, the quality of the time spent as well as quantity is vital.

John is really a great example to all of us. You have firsthand knowledge of how many things keep him busy and yet he makes sure that he books out time every day in his hectic schedule to spend with us. And then he also spends time with us each individually. If I know my husband well enough, I would imagine that he would do that for his managers, employees and with you, Shafik?"

John blushes. "Thanks, Charmaine," he says softly, "You have made my day!"

"Before I forget, Shafik, I will email you an online brain assessment that you can complete before our next visit. We are going to the Neurobix Academy."

"Do you think you will pass your brain test, Mr Muscle," Michaela directs her quirk at Shafik. "What if the professor fails you?"

Shafik laughs out loud. "You can't fail those tests just as much as you can't fail your own blood test. But have you passed yours, Miss Intelligence?"

"Maybe you haven't noticed, but I am not blond. I got 100%!" Michaela deftly answers.

The laughter dies down and the comfortable silence rests among them. John breaks the silence with a more serious question.

"Shafik, you are still very young, and you will be successful. But one day, when you are lying on your deathbed, who would you want beside your bed?"

After a few seconds, Shafik says, "Surely my wife and children that I still need to meet....and the three of you, if you're still alive?"

"I agree. One would want those closest to you by your side. And if they can be there, it often means that you have lived well.

A person can have all the money in the world, but if you have failed at building relationships, what have you lived for? Your greatest legacy will be the relationships you have built with people around you, but especially those closest to you."

With these words, John turns into the filling station to fill up the vehicle with diesel and for the troop to stretch their legs. Before long they are back on the road, teasing each other about the weekend's adventure. John drops Shafik off at his apartment and Shafik thanks them profusely for an exciting and fulfilling weekend.

That night in bed, Shafik feels like the richest man alive. He has spent an adventurous weekend with people close to his heart. Especially that dark haired beauty whose face, sense of humour and beautiful personality he now misses. What a jewel she will be to her future husband...

9. MINING FOR GOLD

The light rain draws curtains over the city as Shafik drives towards Gordon's Bay. Just before the pass, he turns right and follows the sign boards to the Neurobix Academy. Upon seeing the sign board, he imagines his brain doing aerobic exercises. Seems like an apt name for a tutoring centre where they focus on brain assessments and fitness.

As he walks into Café Bella next door to the Academy, he spots John sitting with a steaming cup of coffee in his hand. After ordering his own coffee, Shafik shows John the goals he set out for maintaining three-dimensional health.

John gives Shafik a proud pat on the shoulder. "You're flying, Shafik! Here is your next key."

Shafik takes the key and notices the engraving: **'ENJOY LIFE'**. He slots it in next to the other seven keys. As Shafik looks up, a dark-haired woman walks in. John stands up and greets the woman.

"Shafik, let me introduce you. This is Stephanie Mans, mother of three and innovative director of Neurobix Academy."

While waiting for her tea, Stephanie takes out the results of Shafik's assessment.

"Normally, we send the results and explanations directly to the client, but Prof John asked me to hold back on yours so that we can discuss it together. We live in a time where brain power will be one of the most important determining factors of success. We would like to help you to think better, learn more, and be more creative so that you can have the competitive edge over your competition."

Shafik is all ears. He moves forward in his seat, almost if he wants to make sure that no words fall on the ground. "Who and what does Neurobix focus on, Stephanie?"

Stephanie continues. "We cater for all ages and types of people, Shafik. We help preschoolers to get ready for school; grade 4 children who need to start writing exams; we help children study and give them brain exercises to increase brain fitness at aftercare. We also help grade 9 pupils to choose their subjects for the next year. The assessments and feedback help the students to understand how their brain functions. Some students, after having done the assessments, have even decided to change their courses to ensure they follow a career that aligns with their dreams. Our courses even assist corporate companies with team building, leadership training, emotional intelligence and many other aspects to help them improve their profit margins. We have had marriages take a turn for the better when spouses understand each other and their children better. If we had the time, Shafik, I would have liked to share with you the testimonies of how people's lives have been changed irrevocably after they completed these assessments."

Shafik's face shows his wonder. "It sure seems that you are making a difference, Stephanie!"

"Thank you, Shafik. You have such great potential. An assessment like the one you completed, aims at helping you to develop all of you. That is why we test six drivers that determine your brain functions and 11 intelligence preferences that are unique to you."

For the next half an hour, Stephanie explains to Shafik the function of the two hemispheres in his brain as well as the four quadrants. She shows him his strengths on which he should focus as well as the lesser developed areas. She also shares with him exercises that could help to 'switch on' the less active drivers in his brain to help him reach his potential.

Shafik's brain is spinning with excitement as Stephanie gets up to leave for another appointment. As she walks away, Shafik cannot help but feel a deep sense of appreciation for what he has just learnt about himself. His motivation level to ensure that he develops optimally is sky-high!

John orders another round of coffee for both and picks up on the next subject.

"Today, I think we should have a chat about coaching. Now that you and I understand a bit more how that brilliant brain of yours works, we can tailor our coaching sessions. This is something you need to remember: if you can understand those who work with and for you, it will result in better relationships and better appointments of people in the right positions. The most important aspect though, is that it can help you to help them mine the gold that was deposited in them."

Shafik takes a sip of the steaming hot coffee. "You've used the word 'coaching', John. Does that have the same meaning as the person who coaches an athlete?"

"You're on the right track, Shafik! Coaching is to believe in someone and to empower that person from his or her current position in life, to the place of their dreams. Coaching can help to mine that gold and to maximise your growth. The coach does not make decisions on behalf of you, but will guide you to make quality decisions yourself."

John shifts to the edge of his seat to be closer to Shafik before he continues. "Excellent coaches are good at asking the right questions. They help the person reflect on where they are and where they want to be. They lead people to devise a strategy and action plan for their lives. A good coach will therefore challenge you to think, to get out of your comfort zone, to take up responsibility for your life and to do what needs to be done."

This is a lot for Shafik to take in and for a few moments, he has nothing to say. John has turned his gaze to the fire place and it seems he too is quickly lost in thought, until Shafik breaks the silence.

"Why did you want to share with me these things about coaching, Mister John? I don't want to be a coach. I want to be an entrepreneur. Am I missing something?"

"I appreciate your honesty, Shafik" John is not put off by his honest remark. "I am in no way trying to make a life coach out of you. But I have long ago spotted the gold in you and believe you have what it takes to be successful one day because of your people skills. You can be a giant in business one day. And I would give my all to be your coach to help you reach that pinnacle. I am telling you these things so that you can know where I am leading you to. But I cannot do it for you. We've both seen how unique your brain profile is. And you're the one who will have to put in the work to reach your dreams. Does that make sense, Shafik?"

Shafik's gaze rests on the mug in his hands. "Of course, Mister John." Shafik looks up and his eyes meet his mentor's. "I value who you are and I am eternally grateful to you for this one in a million chance that you have given me."

"Shafik, you do realise there is more to life? Even if you reach all your dreams and it is all you do in life, you will still end up empty in your old age. There is much more to life than just being successful."

Shafik frowns. "What do you mean? I thought that was what we were working towards. Being successful?"

"Of course. But I believe that you will have great impact wherever you move, Shafik. Young people will look up to you and those working with and for you, may want to learn some of your good traits. Maybe God will place it on your heart to also one day impart what you've learned to someone else. And for that reason, it is vitally important that you learn the best coaching skills. Coaching should be a normal part of your life. One of my friends always says that we should be like an air conditioning unit. Wherever we go, we need to change the atmosphere."

"Okay, so you're saying that if I become successful, but have not imparted what I've learnt, there would be no legacy left?"

"Spot on, young man!" John says with shiny eyes now that the penny has dropped for Shafik.

"That makes sense, Mister John. Do you have any ideas how I can master these coaching techniques?"

"I tell you what: if you're interested in doing business with me, I have a proposition for you."

"Mister John, you must know by now that I am open to any business idea!" Shafik replies hastily.

"Here is my plan, Shafik," John says, moving Shafik's notepad and pen closer to him. "If you are prepared to research the best international coaching courses that are available on the internet, I will pay for one such course for you to complete part time. I want you to bring at least three quotations in order of importance to our next session. I also would like to see your motivation for choosing the one above the other."

"That sounds reasonable, Mister John! But where's the catch?"

John smiles. "I was wondering whether you will ask. You will have to do your practical hours at my business with people I choose. I will pay you a full coaching fee, if you're not too expensive! There are a few employees who urgently need coaching help and I cannot get to everyone. Are you in, Shafik?"

"Sounds like a challenging plan. So yes, Mister John, I am in!"

The grumble in Shafik's stomach tells him it's almost lunch time. The morning has flown by so quickly! He is just about to pack away his stationery and assessment results, when John reminds him of their last session.

"I want to organise dinner at a hotel for our last session. This will be our tenth session. I would appreciate it if you can hire a suit for the occasion?"

"Wow, that will certainly be a first for me, Mister John."

"And don't worry about transport, Shafik. I will send someone to pick you up next Saturday at 5pm. Bring an overnight bag and clothes for church the following morning."

"Sounds perfect! Thanks, Mister John. And don't worry about the bill for the coffees. I've got this!"

With that, Shafik gets up and gives John a warm hug.

John cannot help but smile as he sits down behind the wheel of his Toyota. It is the first time that Shafik has offered to pay the bill and the first time he has given John a hug. That is a huge step forward. His love for this young man is growing rapidly and he prays with open eyes as he heads home, "Thank you Father God for the privilege of seeing the transformation in Shafik. Thank you that for him, you only have good and big dreams! You are amazing, Father! In Jesus Name, Amen!"

10. INNER CIRCLE SECRETS

It is just after four o'clock and Shafik is already showered and dressed for the big evening. He wishes he could move time quicker. His black tuxedo fits perfectly, and his black bow-tie looks great against the freshly ironed white shirt. With his new haircut, shining shoes and aftershave, he feels ready and excited for whatever the night may bring.

Just before five, he bounces down stairs to wait for his lift. To his surprise, a white Hummer limousine pulls up at the kerb. Shafik does not move. Surely this cannot be his lift? But then the chauffeur gets out, walks round and opens the passenger door for Shafik. Inside, his eyes adjust to the dim light, and there are three pairs of eyes staring at him with huge smiles. John, Charmaine and Michaela break out laughing when they see his amazement!

Charmaine compliments Shafik on his suit and John pours each a glass of non-alcoholic champagne. "To Shafik!" John says as he raises his glass and winks at his daughter.

Through the tinted windows, Shafik can see that they are not going to the City centre, but more towards the sea. After a short ride, they turn towards the mountain, and drive through an impressive entrance gate. The limousine stops at the entrance to the hotel and two pairs of hands open the passenger doors and help the ladies out.

Shafik looks up and softly reads the sign board: *The Twelve Apostles Hotel*. They walk up the stairs to a big fancy area where dinner is served. Shafik hears the snapping of cameras and is strangely thankful that someone thought to take pictures of them on this big night. As his eyes drink in the opulence, he cannot help but think back to the tin shack where he grew up. What a contrast!

The guests of honour are already seated when they walk in. John introduces Shafik to them one by one. There are three ladies and three men around their table and by the sound of it, they are some of the richest people in Cape Town. But to Shafik's surprise, John's general manager, Mr Davids, is also there. At least one more person that Shafik knows.

Shafik looks over at Michaela. She is looking beautiful in a flowing deep red dress with her pitch-black hair falling softly to her shoulders. He can still smell some of her perfume on his suit from their 'hello hug' when he climbed into the limousine.

John sits at the head of the table, with Charmaine to his left and Michaela to her left. Shafik sits at John's right hand next to Mr Davids. With everyone seated, John lightly taps with the handle of his knife on the table to get everyone's attention. The table quietens down.

"I would like to thank you all for coming tonight to celebrate this big evening with us. I know you are all very busy people. Shafik, have you managed to find out about those online coaching courses?"

Shafik feels a red glow moving up from his neck over his face. He reaches into his right pocket and takes out a piece of paper. He quickly glances around the table and thankfully sees that the other guests have started up their own conversations again.

He unfolds his notes and hands it over to John. John quickly scans and is satisfied with the outcome.

"Great work, Shafik! When you are ready, you can register!"

John regains the group's attention again, and opens the conversation with, "As you may be aware, Shafik and myself have been working on some interesting topics. Tonight, as group, we can discuss the last topic: **the inner circle**. Is there anyone who has some wise words to share?"

A very elegant lady in her late forties, dressed in a midnight blue gown, lifts her right hand ever so slightly, before she speaks. "Shafik, never ever be satisfied with second best. And that goes for the people you associate with too. Go find those people who have high expectations and are not afraid of hard work. That is where you will grow most!"

Now that the ice is broken, someone else jumps right in. "Yes, I agree. Surround yourself with the best people. Winners. Successful people with values and skills that you would want. Self-starters, those who motivate others, loyal supporters and friends."

In her gentle voice, Michaela also contributes. "Shafik, this is what I have learnt from my father. People you are in contact with regularly, will influence your end destination. That is why we must ask ourselves regularly: Who is in my inner circle? What influence do they have on me? Where am I heading to with them around me?"

Shafik nods and is amazed at the wisdom Michaela is exhibiting.

"May I ask something?" Shafik's eyes sweep around the table as he poses his question to the group. "Who are we talking about? Our friends or only work colleagues?"

Charmaine is ready to help. "The inner circle relates to your very close friends, your life partner, and those at work that are close to you. They are the people who live closest to you and with whom you spend the most time."

In his mind, Shafik runs through his list of friends. They are wonderful people and he loves them dearly. But there is not really anyone that jumps out as someone who has high aspirations. And then he looks at John, Charmaine and Michaela. Since he has been in contact with John, and having been visiting regularly with the family, his life has certainly taken a positive turn.

Mr Davids breaks Shafik's train of thought. "Every relationship you are in influences your life either positively or negatively or not at all! If you want to be successful in life, you must question your relationships. The logical choice would be to spend more time with those who have a positive influence on your life!"

"I recall a conversation with Mister John about this: so, it may mean I have to cut out negative people in my life?" Shafik asks.

"Do you remember the little trees in your brain, Shafik" John asks. "It works almost the same with our relationships. If we give those positive relationships in our lives the most attention, it will grow the fastest. If you choose to spend less time with negative people, those 'relationship trees' will later die off."

"And remember, Shafik," Charmaine adds, "We are known by our friends. All of us around this table want to be successful. And we choose to have successful friends. They pull us with them into a successful future. When you have the best people in your circle, they will introduce you to other successful people in their circles. And so we continue to grow in an upwards motion of success."

A man at the other end of the table, whose name Shafik cannot recall, remarks, "I like what John Maxwell says. He believes you have to appoint the best possible people in your management team. It is almost the same as what Jesus did when He appointed the 12 apostles. They were always with Him, and just look at the influence they had on the world. But out of the 12, there were only three who were part of Jesus' inner circle. To get the best possible circle around you, is a win-win situation. You expose yourself to so much new knowledge about the world, business and relationships. It can all influence your positivity and we all know that ninety percent of life is how you look at it!"

The lady in the blue dress, nods her head in affirmation. "I have never met a successful person who spends most of his time with negative people. No, they surround themselves with go-getters with a positive outlook on life."

John puts his hand on Shafik's shoulder. "You have a long-life journey ahead of you, Shafik. Some people will come into your life, and others will go. Some will stay the course. But you are ultimately the only one who can choose who will accompany you on that journey."

Shafik slowly nods his head in agreement.

"May I share something with you about legacy, Shafik?" Mr Davids asks. "Life is like a light wind that blows. Before you know it, it has stopped or shifted. Not one of us knows how long we will walk this earth. That is why we should live in such a way that we leave a legacy for others. Lives that set an example of positive impacts. I want to challenge you to go and write down what you want to be said at your funeral and then, live that way so that it will be said."

The stately lady in the blue dress, adds, "To leave a legacy, is like planting a tree. As the tree grows, it will provide seed so that future generations can plant their own trees. There is one leader who was a sterling example: Myles Munroe. He empowered his leaders to live full lives. A week before his death, he told them, 'I have written all the books I needed to write. I have given each of you the baton. If I should suddenly die, are you ready to run the rest of the race?' And they were ready. Myles and his wife tragically died a week later in an plane crash, but his dream and their legacy lives on."

The impact of this example hangs in the atmosphere above the dinner table. A man in his fifties, who has been quiet most of the evening, directs his gaze and rhetorical questions to Shafik.

"So, young man, how many people are you going to influence in your life? Have you chosen someone in whose life you can duplicate yourself? With how many people are you going to walk a coaching journey so that their lives may be changed forever?"

Somehow, Shafik feels that, although the questions were

directed to him, everyone was thinking about it. John gauges that everyone has said what was in their hearts and he takes the gap.

"A legacy is much more than just ensuring financial provision for your life partner, your children and grandchildren. You must ask yourself whether you have had a positive influence on your community. Are there others who have bought into your vision so that they can take over when you step out of the race of life?"

John reaches into his pocket and Shafik already knows what is to follow.

"Shafik, we are here tonight to handover to you the last two keys and to encourage and bless you on the journey ahead."

Michaela pushes her chair back, walks over to her father, and collects the two small boxes. When she places them in Shafik's hand and he opens them, he notices the engravings: **'GOLD'** and **'CIRCLE'**. He clenches the two keys tightly in his right hand. He feels a bit emotional when he looks up at Michaela, and then at John and Charmaine.

"Thanks...I...I will put them with the others later, because I don't know how to get passed this bow- tie!"

Everyone bursts out laughing and the mood is instantly lightened.

John folds his napkin, pushes his plate back, and stands up. Shafik senses he has got something important to say.

"Shafik, this special circle of people you see here tonight, are the Billionaire Circle. Not all of us are already there, but some are. We are all striving to become billionaires and to have a mighty positive impact on this planet. Long ago, we decided to see each other four times a year, like we are doing tonight. We visit and have a meal together, and we share our successes and motivate each other to greater heights."

Shafik again looks around the table and knows that he would be able to learn from each of them. John continues.

"We have all decided to invite you to be part of this circle. We have long been searching for a tenth person, but struggled to find the right one. You are of course under no obligation and if you decide this is not for you, we will continue to support and love you. You are welcome to let me know what you decide. Take your time!"

John's last word has only just left his lips, when Shafik, fumbling with his hair and almost knocking over the glass of water, jumps up. He quickly regains his composure, and finds all nine people's eyes on him.

"Mister John, my knees feel like jelly. My answer is 'Yes!' How can I give up an opportunity like this? This is my life dream. I don't have as many zeros in my bank balance, but I already feel at home amongst you!"

As Shafik sits down, he almost misses the chair in his haste. And again, he has the group in stitches.

Charmaine is next to stand up. Shafik cannot imagine that there could be anymore surprises, but she and the group have one more.

"Shafik, we would like to give you something to remember this evening. To remind you that we are proud of you. May it be a symbol that you will always be able to spread your wings even further on the winds of success that God wants to give you."

Charmaine walks round, opens Shafik's left hand and places in it a solid gold ring with the head of an eagle engraved upon it. "Put it on the ring finger of your right hand , because the left ring finger we always leave open for something else!" Charmaine says with a beautiful smile and wink.

The rest of the table gets up and gives Shafik a round of

applause. Shyly, he gets up, this time more gracefully, and gratefully acknowledges their support for him. Everyone raises his glass and John leads them in a shout of 'Success!'

As the group wants to return to their seats, John stops them. "Just a moment, please!"

Mr Davids turns to Shafik and stretches out a hand of congratulations. As he takes his hand, Mr Davids announces something Shafik could never have expected.

"The Council of Directors of Global Trading has unanimously decided to offer you the position of deputy general manager. That means that for one year, you will work very closely with me until you have learnt the trade. Should you be successful, you will be appointed as general manager the following year so that I can go and enjoy my pension. Congratulations, Shafik!"

Again, the group applauds him. Shafik's mouth and words have run dry. Through the tears he does however manage to get out some form of a thank you.

"I don't have words. Mister John, as my personal coach and spiritual father, you have helped to turn my life around. And Charmaine and Michaela have become like my own family. Mr Davids, I won't disappoint you. And to the rest of the guests, I trust that I will get to know you much better in the years to come."

The atmosphere is light and soon the starters are served. For the rest of the evening, the guests play musical chairs by moving around to share stories. By 22:00 the last person finishes his coffee and the group greet one another with blessings of a peaceful night's sleep.

Only Shafik and Michaela stays behind and take a walk to the deck area overlooking the ocean. The excitement of the evening has shaken off any tiredness and they are not yet ready for bed.

"So, what do you do to keep yourself busy and what are your future plans, Michaela?" Shafik almost immediately realises he is in coaching mode.

"You ask very personal questions, Mr Muscle!" Michaela teasingly says. "You know that, since the age of 16, I have had my own beauty salon and that I am the bookkeeper at Global Trading?"

"What! No, Michaela, I did not know that. That is impressive for a young lady like yourself. At least I know that I will get to see you regularly since we are now working for the same company!"

"I have always had an interest in business and figures. The one I think I inherited from my father and the other interest from my mother. She was a lecturer in accounting at the university," Michaela clarifies.

"You are a bright bunch! And except for Mauritius, are there any other places you would want to see?"

Michaela thinks it over before she definitively answers. "Yes, I would like to go and dive in the Maldives, see the animal migration in the Serengeti and then also explore the Great Barrier Reef in Australia. How about you, Shafik?"

"Hmmm....your dream places sounds good to me. May I possibly carry your suitcases there?" Shafik jokingly asks.

"You are more than welcome, Shafik." Her serious answer somehow blindsides Shafik and he does not immediately have a sharp, witty answer for her.

Soon, it is almost midnight. Shafik does the responsible thing and politely says, "If we want to be in time for church and still have a bit of rest, we better get to bed, Michaela!"

"May I just see your ring one last time? I have not had a look at the detail engraved on it."

Shafik moves closer and shows her the ring.

"I am really proud of you, Shafik!" And with that, she gives him a quick kiss on the lips.

Shyly, he takes her hand and walks with her to her room.

Shafik is still floating after that kiss and of course the entire evening filled with surprises. He stares at the ceiling. Just before he falls asleep, he allows himself to accept that he is in love with Michaela. The only problem now is that his new boss is her father!

EPILOGUE

A year later, Shafik was appointed as general manager at Global Trading. Three years later, and with tremendous hard work, he became a director at John's company. At that stage, he had also started two of his own businesses that were starting to show great promise.

And he married the boss's daughter, who subsequently became his father-in-law, adding to the list of attributes of mentor, coach and spiritual father. And that is how 'Mister John' became 'Dad'. The legacy of John will now live on forever.

10 MONTH SUCCESS PLAN

Grow and reach success!

This is a ten-month plan where we guide you to optimal growth in the following ten areas of your life. Experience success and financial fulfilment as never before!

Month 1 **The power of thoughts:**
- Brain function assessment
- Programmed for success
- Brain exercises;
- Creative planning

Month 2 **Dynamite words:**
- Power in words
- Affirmations
- Building your forest: growing new neurons

Month 3 **Breaking down old castles:**
- Discover the castles
- Create new brain pathways
- Demolish old castles
- Reach your goals
- How to prioritise

Month 4 **A life of abundance:**
- Wealthy thoughts
- Money and profit
- Billion Dollar thought patterns

Month 5 **Farm with finances**
- Principles of farming
- Sow yourself rich
- Digging for new wells
- Effective budgeting
- Become debt free

Month 6 **Excellent Managers**

- Strategic planning
- Time management
- Dynamic leadership
- Business plans

Month 7 **Winning Entrepreneurs**

- Start your own business
- Legal requirements
- Cash cows
- Calculated risks
- Cash Flow Quadrant
- Midas touch
- Different streams of income
- Successful marketing

Month 8 **Three dimensional health**

- Work/life balance
- Boundaries
- Physical wellbeing
- Will, intellect and emotions
- Relationships: effort, time and imagination
- People-centred living
- Communication
- Constructive conflict management

Month 9 **Mining for gold**

- Heart of a coach
- Unlock potential
- Coaching techniques
- Build your own coaching business

Month 10 **Inner circle secrets**

- Surrounding yourself with winners
- Choose your travel companions
- Planting trees for future generations
- Handover the baton
- Leave a legacy

For more information, visit our website at
www.coachingwinners.biz
or send an email to **francois@coachingwinners.biz**

OTHER BOOKS BY

FRANCOIS ENGELBRECHT

- MIRACLES TODAY: Life Changing Encounters, Supernatural Healings, Divine Breakthroughs.

- RELEASING YOUR DIVINE CALL: Equipping People to Reach Their Destiny and Fulfil Their Divine Call.

- HOW TO PROPHESY: Exciting Activation of Your Prophetic Gift.

Order your copy at **www.amazon.com** (hard copy or Kindle) or through **www.coachingwinners.biz/product-line/**

OTHER BOOKS BY

ELMARI MARAIS

- THRONE ROOM MESSAGES: Collection of poems

- THRONE ROOM MESSAGES II: JOURNEY TO GRACE: Prophetic proclamations through poetry.

Order your copy at **elmari.29@gmail.com**